T0340140

"*Purpose Delivered* is a most important book that, rightly, articulates the urgent case for a reorientation of how many business leaders need to think in order to help capitalism rediscover a better purpose, and with it, more desperately needed legitimacy. But in Alan's case, it is written by someone who was walked the walk and not just talked the talk".

Lord Jim O'Neill, *Chairman Chatham House.*
Formerly chairman Goldman Sachs Asset Management, Commercial Secretary to the UK Treasury

"There is no doubt the case for an organisation to be Purpose-led has never been stronger. In this important book, Alan sets out the ways organisations can enact purpose, including why CEOs need to take ownership of the agenda and the value of metrics that help to evaluate the success of an organisation in delivering on its purpose. A timely and thought provoking read."

Kevin Ellis, *Chairman PricewaterhouseCoopers*

"Just imagine if each individual, community, business and government truly lived a 'purpose' that has benefit to society, with integrity...sounds like a system with compound positive interest! A dream, or an intent that needs a plan? Here we have an excellent analytical framework, a case study multinational and illuminating examples from personal CEO experience that demonstrate the way forward for us and for business. Thank you, Alan."

Gail Klintworth, *Chair Integrity Action.*
Formerly, Global Chief Sustainability Officer Unilever

"... informed, insightful and challenging... it should be read by all CEO's, advisers and investors for effectively establishing and future proofing viable and sustainable companies of the future."

John Handley, *Chairman portfolio of private equity owned companies*

"As business migrates its rationale from a primary focus on shareholder value to embrace wider society goals, to include the environment, employees, suppliers and customers, a blue print for 'How' is critically needed. In his book, Dr Barlow, provides the guiding principles and route map to achieve this. And, more importantly, shows how he, as a CEO, applied them. I particularly liked the concept of developing a ranking index for FTSE / NYSE companies in terms of the extent to which they are purpose-driven. This is a must read and is a major contribution to this subject area".

Eric Anstee, *Pleural Non-Executive Director.*
Formerly, CEO of The Institute for Chartered Accountants in England & Wales

"As becoming 'purpose-led' goes mainstream, the business focus is shifting from "why bother" to "how to do this well". The core of this timely and insightful book is a powerful worked example, showing the steps a committed and visionary CEO took over five years to put purpose into practice in a challenging context. With a wealth of practical illustrations of dilemmas and decisions, and using Blueprint for Better Business's Five principles as an external benchmark, the book illuminates how taking purpose seriously is both a personal and organisational challenge, and demonstrates the amazing difference it can make – to the benefit of the business, society and the people involved.

Charles Wookey, *CEO Blueprint for Better Business*

"Alan's CEO practitioner experience in how to deliver a purpose-driven business is clearly demonstrated, analytically and practically, in his book. When presenting to our MBA students, he opens their eyes to the challenges and returns from delivering a purpose-defined company. He is an ideal educator for the new generation of leaders of what business should be: responsible, accountable and caring."

Ewa Maciejewski, *Vice Director University of St Gallen Business School, Switzerland*

"When the dominant neo-liberal system is assaulted, the 'company with a purpose' brings hope. Alan's book demonstrates concretely why and how. Sharing his experience as a very effective leader, his book illustrates how profiting through heightened integrity contributes to the common good and delivers for all stakeholders. The book makes explicit the model and the values upon which is built a 'company with a purpose'; and, it is ground-breaking in demonstrating clearly 'how' to implement an effective transformation, and how to make the difficult but unavoidable trade-offs. A very timely work for all enlightened leaders who want to walk the talk."

Henri-Claude de Bettignies, *Emeritus Professor INSEAD Business School, France*

"... a critically important strategic and practical guide to doing the right thing for the right reason for society, while also ensuring corporate financial sustainability ... demonstrates a practical business model for the "how to", with key components and steps to be taken ... with financial and non-financial metrics for leadership to monitor and review performance in delivering the company's purpose ... I wish every CEO and Board Chair on the planet would heed this advice – imagine what a difference that would make in the world."

Denise McNerney, *President American Association for Strategic Planning, CEO iBossWell Inc*

"For company boards, delivering purpose is becoming a requirement, not a nice-to-have. The dominant values in society are changing as millennials are gaining political and economic traction at the expense of boomers. The challenge for company boards is how to define and run a purpose-defined company when purpose goes beyond financial returns. Impact investors, and the ESG movement, have not yet found the answer. In this book, Alan Barlow sets out both a practical framework for defining a purpose-led company across four types of capital that impact investors would recognise. He also, importantly, shows how to operationalise that framework in practice in the way that business processes are implemented, decisions are taken and transparency is provided to all stakeholders. This is an important contribution that should be read by all company boards."

Dr Richard Foster, *External member of the Investment Board University of Cambridge. Formerly, Managing Director Morgan Stanley*

"The shareholder maximisation model is now broken. Alan makes a powerful case for purpose-driven companies. And, based on his CEO experience, he sets out and demonstrates a practical business model on how to make it happen. This is a book whose time has come. A must read."

J. Rajagopal, *CEO & executive coach. Formerly, Executive Vice President Tata Consultancy Services. India*

"Alan Barlow's Purpose Delivered couldn't be more timely and useful … is timely because expectations for corporate purpose have intensified amidst the multiple disruptions that challenge business to contribute more directly to society. It's useful because it explains and demonstrates the why, what and how as matters both of principle and practice. Alan Barlow is a reliable, credible guide because he has delivered the goods – for business and society – as a successful CEO."

Bennett Freeman, *Principal Bennett Freeman Associates. Formerly, U.S. Deputy Assistant Secretary of State for Democracy, Human Rights and Labor*

"This is rare: not only a book on corporate purpose that majors on the 'how', but one based on lived experience. Alan draws effectively on his CEO career to demonstrate the case for a new core competence needed to deliver purpose, a competence based around the concept of 'heightened integrity'. The book is full of pragmatic examples and tools, and enlivened by anecdotes."

Sam Baker, *Lead partner Monitor Deloitte EMEA strategy consulting practice*

Purpose Delivered

Going beyond the why and what of purpose-led business, this book sets out an innovative business model of how to lead and operate a company to deliver its purpose.

Western capitalism is in crisis due to the growing disconnect between business and society, and there are growing calls for a shift from the primacy of shareholder value to the primacy of purpose. But there is a paucity of codified best practice for how CEOs should go about making this shift. Enter Alan Barlow: a CEO practitioner who demonstrates with analytical rigor and evidence-based argument a business model for how CEOs can actually deliver a purpose-defined company that yields both bigger benefits for society and bigger profits for the business.

Current and aspiring business leaders and executives will benefit from not only this new business model but also a fully documented route map for monitoring and reviewing successful impact, and highly focused non-financial and financial metrics for benchmarking. Completing the loop for 'company purpose' means that business can become a force for good for society.

Alan Barlow, formerly CEO, multinational chemical engineering group; Director, FTSE 100/NYSE listed energy group; and Partner, PricewaterhouseCoopers. He has over 25 years' P&L experience encompassing Europe, the Americas, Asia Pacific, the Middle East and India.

Purpose Delivered

Bigger Benefits for Society and
Bigger Profits for Business –
A CEO's Experience

Alan Barlow

Routledge
Taylor & Francis Group

NEW YORK AND LONDON

First published 2021
by Routledge
605 Third Avenue, New York, NY 10158

and by Routledge
2 Park Square, Milton Park, Abingdon, Oxon, OX14 4RN

Routledge is an imprint of the Taylor & Francis Group, an informa business

© 2021 Alan Barlow

The right of Alan Barlow to be identified as author of this work has been asserted by him in accordance with sections 77 and 78 of the Copyright, Designs and Patents Act 1988.

All rights reserved. No part of this book may be reprinted or reproduced or utilised in any form or by any electronic, mechanical, or other means, now known or hereafter invented, including photocopying and recording, or in any information storage or retrieval system, without permission in writing from the publishers.

Trademark notice: Product or corporate names may be trademarks or registered trademarks, and are used only for identification and explanation without intent to infringe.

Library of Congress Cataloging-in-Publication Data
Names: Barlow, Alan, 1947 December 28– author.
Title: Purpose delivered : bigger benefits for society and bigger profits for business - a CEO's experience / Alan Barlow.
Description: New York, NY : Routledge, 2021. | Includes bibliographical references and index.
Identifiers: LCCN 2020053686 (print) | LCCN 2020053687 (ebook)
Subjects: LCSH: Leadership. | Executive ability. | Success in business.
Classification: LCC HD57.7 .B36638 2021 (print) | LCC HD57.7 (ebook) | DDC 658.4/2—dc23
LC record available at https://lccn.loc.gov/2020053686
LC ebook record available at https://lccn.loc.gov/2020053687

ISBN: 9780367757823 (hbk)
ISBN: 9780367757816 (pbk)
ISBN: 9781003163978 (ebk)

Typeset in Sabon
by codeMantra

Contents

List of Illustrations   *xi*
Preface   *xiii*
Acknowledgements   *xv*
About the Author   *xvii*

1   THE CHALLENGE: Responding to the increasing
    disconnect between business and society   1

2   THE '*WHY*'?: The need to redefine the nature and
    purpose of a company   7

3   THE '*WHAT*'?: A paradigm shift from the primacy of
    shareholder value to the primacy of purpose   12

4   THE '*HOW*'?: Implement the 'Heightened Integrity Model':   17
    Governance, delivery, and performance 18
    Heightened integrity: the hub of the model 20
    Heightened integrity model 22

5   DEMONSTRATION: Application of the model to the
    case study multinational corporation   26
    The case study corporation 26
    Enabling subprocesses: 28
        Purpose 28
        Stakeholders 31
        Integrity /compliance 33
    Delivery subprocesses: 36
        Leadership 36
        Staff 45
        Feedback 51

6   VERIFICATION: Successful benchmarking of the
    model against third party best practice: 56
    Purpose: Behavioural principles: 56
      Being a responsible and responsive employer 57
      Being honest and fair with customers and suppliers 66
      Being a guardian for future generations 71
      Being a good citizen 74
    Purpose: Great place to work 78
    Purpose: Measurable business payoffs 80
    Wider applicability of the model 82

7   DELIVERED: Bigger benefits for society and bigger
    profits for business   86

8   RECONNECTING: A growing range of programmes
    and legislation for reconnecting business with society: 90
    Believer companies 90
    Believer proclaimers 90
    Believer investors 91
    Purpose-based legislation 92
    Third party assessment and ranking 93
    Company purpose: Root cause and leadership 95

9   RESOLUTION: For society, and for a company   99
    For Society 99
    For a Company 100

    Appendix: The Group's business model   103
    Index   111

Illustrations

Figures

4.1	The 'Heightened Integrity Model'	23
5.1	The Group's annual communications programme	47
6.1	Overview of the Knowledge Bank	59
8.1	Company purpose: Its root cause	95
A.1	Overview of the Group's market sectors and growth drivers	104
A.2	Fundamentals for delivering the Group's purpose and vision	107
A.3	The Group's portfolio business model	109
A.4	The Group's two-game strategy	110

Tables

5.1	Transformation of staff terms and conditions	32
5.2	Rationale of the code of values	35
5.3	Rating of processes for closing the feedback loop	53

Preface

My reason for writing this book – as a capitalist with a social conscience – is to assist in getting the following message out.

Capitalism must change. It is in crisis because there is increasing disconnect between business and society, with global crises such as environmental issues and social inequality. Business must become a force for good for society, and be profitable.

There is a need to rethink the nature and purpose of a company. There has to be a paradigm shift from primacy of shareholder value to primacy of purpose. There is now a well-documented case for the '*Why*' companies should be purpose-driven and the '*What*' they should do.

However, there is an important gap in the '*purpose*' company agenda: A lack of evidence-based business models as guides for the '*How*' CEOs should deliver the pre-defined purpose of their company as well as being highly profitable.

The book puts the CEO at centre stage for the actual delivery of a company's defined purpose. To this end, an evidence-based model is put forward for the '*How*' CEOs deliver a company's defined purpose – the '*Heightened Integrity Model*'. It is demonstrated by application to a multinational corporation where I'm its CEO. The model is verified by benchmarking it against best practice from several independent third parties of what is expected from a purpose-driven company. This also confirms its wider applicability beyond a case study.

Purpose Delivered is ground-breaking. It provides stakeholders, boards, chairpersons and CEOs with the following:

- An evidence-based business model demonstrated for how a purpose-defined company can deliver bigger benefits for society and bigger profits for business.
- A documented process for monitoring and reviewing the extent to which their CEO is actually successful in executing the company's defined purpose.
- A highly focused set of non-financial and financial metrics for assessing the extent to which companies are purpose-driven.

The loop is therefore complete for '*company purpose*'. In addition to the '*Why*' and the '*What*' to do, there is now a business model for the '*How*' CEOs can actually deliver a company's defined purpose. Business thus becomes a force for good for society. It is in the self-interest of business to be purpose-driven.

I'm using the book as a basis for briefings and speaking engagements to various stakeholders in order to get the message out.

Royalties from sales of the book go to the charity 'Integrity Action', where I am a trustee.

Acknowledgements

A number of people kindly assisted me in various ways which has resulted in much greater clarity of argument and nuance of exposition of my proposition, its demonstration and verification, and hence its rigor.

Professor Colin Mayer (author of *Prosperity*, 2018) kindly let me have sight of several pre-publication chapters of his book, following discussion of my presentation to MBA students at Said Business School University of Oxford, which proved to be highly invaluable. The very useful exchange with Charles Wookey, CEO of Blueprint for Better Business, prompted my looking at how the behaviours in my case study illustrate its five principles of a purpose-driven company. Highly constructive and incisive comments have been received on an earlier draft from Professor Alex Edmans (of the London Business School and author of *Grow the Pie*, 2020) and Sam Baker (partner, leader of the Monitor Deloitte strategy consulting practice).

In addition, thanks go to John Berriman and David Parish, my former colleagues at PricewaterhouseCoopers, for their encouragement and comments on an earlier draft of the book, and to Fiona Carter for invaluable editing support.

Special thanks also go to my former colleagues at Hamworthy Combustion Group (the Group), which is the case study multinational corporation. They delivered the transformation of the Group for it become a recognised world leader, and hence the basis of the book.

Finally, extra special thanks to my wife, Lindsey, for her continuing encouragement and support during the period of writing the book.

As ever, limitations and errors are my responsibility alone.

About the Author

Alan Barlow has some 25+ years of international experience, with extensive P&L responsibilities for multi-country operations in Europe, the Americas, Asia Pacific, the Middle East, East Africa and the subcontinent of India.

His executive career is wide ranging and includes a range of different ownership types: partner at PricewaterhouseCoopers, which included five years' residence in the Asia Pacific region; director of a FTSE-100/ NYSE-listed integrated energy group; and CEO of a private equity-owned mid-cap multinational chemical engineering group – which provides the case study for the book.

Currently, Alan is a board member and trustee of the charity Integrity Action and has a portfolio of charity trusteeships. He has a doctorate degree in economics from Oxford University.

He is regularly invited as a speaker on how to deliver a Purposeful / Responsible business. He is also the author of *Profiting from Integrity* (Routledge 2018).

Chapter 1

THE CHALLENGE

Responding to the Increasing Disconnect between Business and Society

Capitalism must change. It is in crisis. There is increasing disconnect between business and society, with global issues such as environmental issues and social inequality.

The libertarian beliefs of the baby boomer generation on company's maximising shareholder value, as promulgated by Milton Friedman's free market capitalism, are under considerable threat. Millennials are now increasingly in the driving seat: They think differently, act differently and have different values; they are the largest single group eligible to vote in many OECD countries; their wealth is growing; and they believe that measuring corporate success predominantly by financial performance is insufficient. Shareholder value for a single constituency must give way to stakeholder value where stakeholders cover multiple identity groups.

For many stakeholders, the situation can variously be summarised as follows: corruption, widespread; compliance, inadequate; governance, not delivering; corporate social responsibility, patchy; ethics, disconnected; and company codes of conduct, vacuous. In response, there are increasing legislative (e.g. UK Corporate Governance Code 2017, Section 172 of the UK Companies Act) and investor (e.g. Fink 2018) requirements on companies to report their business performance in terms of management intangibles, such as purpose and culture; engagement with employees, suppliers and customers; and making a positive contribution to society.

Some major private investors are recognising publicly that there is a vital need for a change from shareholder primacy. Ray Dalio, founder of Bridgewater Associates (a hedge fund with £125bn of assets) put it as follows: *"The income / wealth / opportunity gap is leading to dangerous social and political divisions that threaten our cohesive fabric and capitalism itself. If there is no reform, we will have great conflict and some form of revolution"* (Dalio 2019).

Consequently, it is increasingly recognised that there is a need to re-think the nature and purpose of a company. It calls for a paradigm shift from primacy of shareholder value to primacy of purpose. The case for the '*Why*' companies should exist and be 'purpose'-based and the '*What*' this requires of them is now well documented (e.g. The Big Innovation Centre 2016; A Blueprint for Better Business 2017; Mayer 2018; Edmans 2020).

However, there is a big and important gap in the 'purpose' company agenda. The gap is the response to the subsequent question of the '*How*' to deliver a purpose-defined company. There is a paucity of evidenced-based business models to serve as guidance for the '*How*' CEOs should actually go about delivering the pre-defined purpose of their company that is also highly profitable.

The specific challenge now outstanding is one of putting forward, demonstrating and verifying an innovative business model for company boards, their chairpersons, CEOs and leadership teams to adopt and implement for delivering their company's defined purpose.

For delivery of the '*How*', the focus here is necessarily on the CEO, who is at the centre stage for the actual delivery of a company's defined purpose. It is the CEO, under good corporate governance, who has the delegated executive authority, responsibility and accountability to deliver a board's defined purpose for its company; as, for example, is the case for its strategy. The company's board and its chairperson then occupy a pivotal stewardship/trustee role for monitoring and reviewing that the company's defined purpose is being implemented and that long-term value creation is being delivered.

The implementation of a company's defined purpose for long-term value creation requires the introduction of a radical new core competence. There has to be a shift in the culture and behaviour of how the company is led, operated and hence how things are done throughout the entirety of the organisation. This, in turn, requires the definition and implementation of a new core business process model. The proposed innovative model is based on a culture of leading and operating a company with heightened integrity. It must pervade the entire activities of a company in order to deliver its purpose, as defined and adopted by its board.

The need to redefine the nature and purpose of a company is the subject of Chapter 2 (The '*Why?*'). As based on a brief literature review, the '*Why*' question is responded to in terms of the following: The fundamental reason a company exists; how its purpose is determined; how it requires a fundamental change in mindset; how it is a case of growing the pie and not a zero-sum game between business and society; how there is a need to operate on a higher ethical plane; how goods must do good and services serve; and how it does 'good' and does not do 'bad'.

Chapter 3 then considers, again based on a brief review of the literature, the '*What?*' a purpose-defined company must do. There are broadly two emerging schools of thought of the '*What*' to do for a company to be purpose-driven:

- One largely sees the need for legislative changes to national industrial policies with respect to governance and reporting, as promulgated by The Big Innovation Centre[1] and Professor Colin Mayer.
- The other focuses more on actions required by companies themselves, as prescribed by Blueprint for Better Business and Professor Alex Edmans.

There is, notwithstanding these apparent differences in philosophy, considerable cohesion of core message: the imperative of company purpose over maximising shareholder value, and that company profits result and flow from its purpose. It requires a paradigm shift from primacy of shareholder value to the primacy of purpose.

Chapter 4, "The '*How?*': Implement the 'Heightened Integrity Model'", sets out the proposed model for how CEOs can actually deliver a purpose-defined company along with superior profitability.

It encompasses the following:

- The rationale for the six subprocesses that make up the business model and their dynamic relationships.
- The three enabling subprocesses of Purpose statement (Be big, bold, ambitious, authentic, inspirational and practical); Stakeholders (Identify and value the specific connection that matters – Its people); and Integrity/compliance (Embody an integrity and compliance ethos in the business).
- The three delivery subprocesses of Leadership (Ensure leadership's moral compass is seen to demonstrate the right tone from the top); Staff (Deliver radical staff engagement and communication); and Feedback (Proactively close the feedback loop between leaders and the company's people).

The rationale is presented for why heightened integrity is at the hub of the model as the modus operandi of leading and operating a company to deliver its defined purpose. Additionally, two critical relationships are explained that are pivotal for successful realisation of a company's purpose. They are the interaction between the board's chairperson and its CEO, and the interaction between middle-level management and a company's people, with the latter driving performance.

Chapter 5 demonstrates the application of the model to a case study multinational corporation (a chemical engineering group), where the author is brought in by the Group's new owners (a private equity house) as CEO to grow the corporation and its profits for its subsequent sale.

Following a brief description of the case study corporation, each of the model's six subprocesses is considered in turn. The in-principle application of each subprocess for companies per se and for the case study corporation is set out. This is followed by the application of each subprocess to the Group by demonstrating with direct examples of how what is done and why in the Group to deliver its defined purpose.

The 'Heightened Integrity Model' is then verified by successfully benchmarking its application to the case study corporation against three sets of leading third-party best practice (Chapter 6). They are:

• The set of five behavioural principles a purpose company must comply with as laid out by the UK-based think-tank Blueprint for Better Business (2017).
• The definition and attributes of 'a great place to work' as defined by the US-based company Great Place to Work Institute (Edmans 2012).
• The set of nine measurable business payoffs that a purpose company must meet as laid out by the UK-based think-tank, The Big Innovation Centre (2016).

Greater veracity for the business model's robustness and the rigor of its case study application is therefore gained.

Moreover, the benchmarking also serves to demonstrate the wider applicability of the model beyond a single case study. The three independent sets of third-party best practice, drawn on for the benchmarking, are grounded on survey evidence from a wide range of companies from all sectors of activity. The chapter thus concludes with an evidence-based argument as to why the model has wider applicability.

It is noted that the *'five behavioural principles'* and *'nine measurable business payoffs'* are subsequently employed as financial and non-financial metrics for how stakeholders, boards, chairpersons and CEOs can assess the extent to which companies are purpose-driven.

With respect to presenting the results of the actual delivery of the case study corporation's purpose (Chapter 7: "DELIVERED: Bigger benefits for society and bigger profits for business"), this is demonstrated in terms of integrated business reporting. High-level results are presented for each category of business capital: natural capital, intellectual capital, human capital, social capital, and financial capital – with profits being at an 18 per cent compound average growth rate. Such a comprehensive and systematic body of results also provides further evidence-based argument in support of the model's rigor and robustness for how to execute a company's defined purpose.

It concludes that the successful implementation of the 'Heightened Integrity Model' by a purpose-defined company does result in long-term sustainable performance for the economy and the company. Bigger benefits to society and bigger profits for the business are delivered.

Chapter 8 summarises the growing range and number of programmes and legislation underway for companies to adopt purposefulness in the quest for business to reconnect with society. Several of their limitations are also noted.

An additional and a very different approach is also put forward. It is one of publicly ranking major companies (e.g. FTSE and/or NYSE listed companies) by the extent to which they demonstrate delivery of a purpose defined company agenda. It is argued that for companies with a poor ranking, in having a branding and reputational impact (i.e. in being 'named and shamed'), this could then lead to some laggard major companies modifying their behaviour and pursuing a more purpose-driven corporate agenda.

The root cause of 'Company purpose' is set out. It is the entwinement of the intergenerational shift in values between the 'Baby Boomers' of the 1980s / 90s and the 'Millennials' of the 2000 onwards, and over broadly the same period the shift in the basis of company investment valuation from tangible to intangible assets. Consequently, a company's people are the intrinsic source of a company's investment value, and the company has accordingly to operate on a high ethical plane i.e. being led and operated by CEOs with heightened integrity.

The final chapter (9: "RESOLUTION: For society, and for a company") concludes that for society, a portfolio of programmes and legislation is required for reconnecting business with society; no single silver bullet resolution can be expected.

For individual companies with a defined purpose, it proposes that they should adopt and implement the innovative business model: The 'Heightened Integrity Model'.

Additionally, the business model provides stakeholders, company boards, their chairpersons, their CEOs and other company leaders with the following:

- A demonstrated methodology for how to lead and operate a company so that it delivers its defined purpose, in terms of bigger benefits for society and bigger profits for business.
- A fully documented process (by applying precise behavioural principles and operational metrics) for monitoring and reviewing the extent to which their CEO is actually successful in executing the company's defined purpose.
- A highly focused set of non-financial and financial metrics for assessing the extent to which companies are purpose-driven.
- An illustration of the application of integrated business reporting for a purpose-driven company.

- A recommendation and innovative approach of ranking say FTSE/NYSE listed companies by the extent to which they are purpose-driven, thereby 'naming and shaming' laggards which would have branding and reputational impact and possibly lead to them upping their game.

The loop is therefore complete for 'company purpose'. In addition to the 'Why' and the 'What' to do, there is now a business model for the 'How' to actually deliver a company's defined purpose. Business then becomes a force for good for society. Inefficient markets become more efficient.

Note

1 This is the focus of its first report which is subsequently modified in its later work with an emphasis on changes in executive pay and investor engagement, see: https://alexedmans.com/the-purposeful-company

References

A Blueprint for Better Business (2017). "Five principles of a purpose company". A Blueprint for Better Business. London.

Dalio, R. (2019). "Why and how capitalism needs to be reformed". LinkedIn, posted 4 April.

Fink, L. (2018). "Letter to CEOs". BlackRock. www. blackrock.com accessed 7 February 2019.

Edmans, A. (2012). The link between job satisfaction and firm value with implications for corporate social responsibility. Academy of Management Perspective, 26(4), pp. 1–19.

Edmans, A. (2020). "Grow the Pie: How great companies deliver purpose and profit". Cambridge University Press, Cambridge.

Mayer, C. (2018). "Prosperity: Better business makes greater good". Oxford University Press, Oxford.

The Big Innovation Centre (2016). "The purposeful company". Big Innovation Centre. London.

UK Corporate Governance Code (December, 2017). Section 172, UK Companies Act, 2006.

Chapter 2

THE 'WHY?'

The Need to Redefine the Nature and Purpose of a Company

Companies must pursue a purpose-defined agenda. This is in response to the growing disconnect between business and society. That is, there is a growing groundswell advocating that business must become a force for good for society.

In defining a company's purpose, the fundamental question is the '*Why*' should a company exist. As presented in Box 2.1, several leading think-tanks and internationally recognised academics have a considerable commonality of definition for 'purpose', with – as could be expected – several nuances (e.g. The Big Innovation Centre 2016; A Blueprint for Better Business 2017; Mayer 2018; Edmans 2020).

A specific nuance is that whilst The Big Innovation Centre, Blueprint for Better Business and Mayer explicitly emphasise an ethos of utilitarianism with respect to a company's behaviour per se, Edmans's focus is largely in terms of there being a bigger pie for society to share.

Drawing directly from these works and their words:

- A company's purpose is the fundamental why it exists; its reason for being; what it aspires to become; and what it contributes to society. Profits are not the purpose of a company per se but must be made for the company to survive. Purpose is the instrument for the attainment of profit. Profit is the derivative of company purpose.
- A company's purpose is determined by asking the following questions: What is its value proposition? What value is it seeking to provide, who to and over what time period? A purpose-driven company delivers goods and services that serve a societal or economic need in a manner that creates long-term sustainable performance. A company lives its purpose through its set of values and beliefs that establish the way in which it operates. Purpose is the particular and distinctive way in which a company serves society and builds a stronger business in a sustainable manner. There is a need to respect each individual and promote their fulfilment in contributing to society; not treat people as a means of production and a 'something'

but as a 'someone'. This then builds up trust between people, and between business and society. A purpose statement must be more than a mission statement. It has to explain how a company's business aims to benefit society.

• A purpose company does 'good' and it does not do 'bad' for future as well as for current generations in a sustainable manner. A purpose company provides goods that are good and services that serve. It lifts companies onto higher ethical planes. It generates a bigger pie to share; it is not a zero-sum game.

Company purpose requires a fundamental change in mindset.

A company's purpose statement should be big, bold, ambitious, authentic, inspirational and practical. It has to resonate with the company's people (and other stakeholders) at every level in order to be arresting.

By way of illustration, Box 2.2 provides the purpose statements of two widely applauded purpose-driven companies: Unilever (a consumer goods company) and GSK (a pharmaceutical company). They demonstrate how social and environmental outcomes link back to their purpose. For information, the purpose of the case study corporation (a multinational chemical engineering group) is presented in Box 2.3, with the discussion of it being the subject of Chapter 5.

Box 2.1 Defining Company Purpose

• The Big Innovation Centre (2016) defines company purpose in terms of the following: ... it lifts companies onto higher ethical planes ... is the reason for it being ... it defines its existence, its contribution to society ... it determines its goals and strategy ... underlying it is a set of values and beliefs that establish the way in which the company operates ... the purpose must be sufficiently compelling ... inspiring to invigorate all members of the company's community (i.e. external relates to customers; internal relates to employees; societal relates to recognition of communities and companies in having a mutuality of interests; moral relates to contributing to the betterment of the world in which we live, both future as well as current generations) ... it must involve big and bold ambitions ... definition in these terms is the source of competitive differentiation.

• Blueprint for Better Business (2017) defines company purpose in terms of the following: ... goods that do good and services that serve ... the fundamental reason that the company exists ...

- businesses are more successful when there is a connection between the purpose of the business, the benefit to society and to all other stakeholders (employees, customers, suppliers, investors) ... dividing it into a purpose that serves society and respects the dignity of people ensures that the company creates long-term sustainable performance ... should describe why the business exists and how it benefits society rather than just a description of what the business does ... it needs to be authentic as well as inspiring and practical ... the purpose is a long-term aspiration and sense of direction.
- Mayer (2018) defines company purpose in terms of the following: ... does 'good' and does not do 'bad' ... the instrument for the attainment of profit ... profit is the derivative purpose ... purpose first, the rest will follow ... purpose is the reason why something is created, exists and is done, what it aspires to become ... the corporation is not just to make profits ... it is to do things that improve problems confronting us as customers, communities, suppliers, shareholders, employees and retirees ... determine corporate purpose by asking what is its value proposition, what value is it seeking to provide, to whom and over what time period .... purpose is the reason for the creation and existence of what it aspires to become.
- Edmans (2020) defines company purpose in terms of the following: ... generating a bigger pie to share, not a zero-sum game ... an enterprise must live its purpose ... it is related its members – who it exists for (i.e. which members and enterprise it wishes to serve) and why it exists (its reason for being) ... the who is based on the principle of materiality, that is, which stakeholders are material to the firm (i.e. business materiality, which generates superior returns to investors), and which stakeholders in the firm it is particularly concerned about (i.e. intrinsic materiality, which is a source of passion for leaders and colleagues).

Box 2.2 Purpose Statements: Unilever and GSK

- Unilever's purpose statement (consumer goods sector):
  Our purpose is to make sustainable living commonplace. With brands that combine superior experiences, bold innovation and a strong sustainable living purpose. With brands that regenerate nature, fight climate change and conserve resources for future generations.

A belief that sustainable business drives superior performance lies at the heart of the Unilever compass – our strategy to create long-term value for our stakeholders.

Our vision is to be the global leader in sustainable business. We will demonstrate how our purpose-led, future-fit business model drives superior performance, consistently delivering financial results in the top third of our industry.

- GSK's purpose statement (pharmaceutical sector):

GSK's mission is to improve the quality of human life by enabling people to do more, feel better, live longer. To achieve this mission we are adapting our business model and pursuing a strategy that delivers sustainable performance through innovation and expanding access, driven by our values.

Commitments: For GSK, how we deliver success is just as important as what we achieve. Ensuring our values are embedded in our business is a priority. In 2012 we developed 23 forward-looking commitments across the four areas of our responsible business approach – Health for all, Our behaviour, Our people, Our planet.

Box 2.3 The Case Study Group's Purpose (Chemical Engineering Sector)

- We contribute to a healthier environment for society and become a guardian of the environment for future generations.
- We benefit society with products and services that result in cleaner air and reduced depletion of natural resources in a long-term sustainable manner.
- We provide technical solutions for reducing the adverse environmental impact of companies operating predominantly in the global, dynamic and generally noxious downstream oil and gas sectors.
- We deliver world leading, cost-effective combustion burners and related services to reduce emissions and increase fuel efficiency with absolute safety for
  - downstream oil and gas companies in the flares, petrochemicals and the marine sectors; and
  - hot water and steam raising applications in the industrial, agriculture/food processing, power plants and marine sectors.

References

A Blueprint for Better Business (2017). *ibid.*
Edmans, A. (2020). *ibid.*
GSK website, accessed 23 July 2020.
Mayer, C. (2018). *ibid.*
The Big Innovation Centre (2016). *ibid.*
Unilever web site, accessed 23 July 2020.

Chapter 3

THE 'WHAT?'

A Paradigm Shift from the Primacy of Shareholder Value to the Primacy of Purpose

For the '*What*' to do for a company to be purpose-driven, two broad schools of thought are increasingly evident. One largely sees the need for legislative changes to national industrial policies with respect to governance and reporting. The other focuses more on actions by companies themselves. Both schools are founded largely on evidence-based argument.

Whilst over-simplifying, their relative differences are based on differing philosophies. In brief, The Big Innovation Centre's (2016) menu of policy options is interventionist leaning; Mayer's (2018) book largely proposes how capitalism needs to change with significant changes in legislation and reporting being put forward. In contrast, the thrust of Edmans's (2020) book is that capitalism can change itself; and Blueprint for Better Business's (2017) principles of a purpose-driven company are largely based on doing good per se.

There is, notwithstanding these apparent differences, considerable cohesion of core message:

- The imperative of company purpose over maximising shareholder value.
- Company profits result and flow from its purpose.
- The need for a paradigm shift from the primacy of shareholder value to the primacy of purpose.

There are, not unexpectedly, significant variations of prognosis of the '*What*' needs to be done to engender business being a force for good for society.

The Big Innovation Centre's (2016) – a UK-based not-for-profit think-tank – policy report addresses 'purpose' largely from the perspective of how to build a strong, domestically owned corporate sector that creates sustainable social and economic value for the UK. This is in response to an under-performing UK economy that has fewer and declining numbers of such companies and where the UK has a poor record on investment, productivity and innovation. Consequently, and in a world where intangible assets dominate, its proposition is that central to success is the pursuit of a deeply defined corporate purpose. To achieve this, it cogently promotes a comprehensive range of policy options for reform in the UK. These range from business implementation and remuneration, corporate governance and commitment devices to block-holding, monitoring and engagement, and strengthening the capabilities of asset owners, to reverse the decline of equity ownership – many of which would require changes in legislation.

The Big Innovation Centre also sets out nine measurable business payoffs that should be expected from a company being led and operated with purpose. The metrics are superior share price performance; improved accounting and operational performance; lower cost of capital; more valuable innovation; improved recruitment, retention and motivation of employees; less adversarial industrial relations; larger firm size and decentralisation; smaller regulatory fines; and greater resilience in the face of external shocks. These performance metrics are drawn on in Chapter 6 as further verification, via benchmarking such best practice, of the proposed core business process model and its application to the case study company in having actually delivered a purpose-driven company. They are also drawn on to illustrate that the proposed model has wider applicability beyond a single case study.

Mayer (2018), similar to The Big innovation Centre, also largely addresses how to rectify the continuing under-performance of the UK economy. He argues the need for a fundamental reassessment of regulation and the requirement of incorporating corporate purpose into corporate law. He states that legislation *"should require companies to articulate their purposes, incorporate them in their articles of association, and above all demonstrate how they credibly commit to the delivery of purpose"* (p. 23).

He puts forward a template of required policy changes in terms of 'governance' and 'performance' so as to ensure that purpose is at the heart of a company. Under governance, he provides a set of principles to rebalance a corporation's focus from financial capital (i.e. primacy of shareholder value and profit maximisation) at the cost of sacrificing the returns from the other forms of capital. With respect to 'performance', Mayer recommends fundamental changes in principles of accounting that have not been fully recognised to date. These relate to integrated reporting on the six forms of capital: financial, human, social, material, intellectual and natural. (These forms of business capital are returned to later in Chapter 7). Mayer's overriding message is that with re-invention of the corporation, business can become a force for societal good. That would restore trust in corporations by society, which he sees as the key to future prosperity.

In sharp contrast to The Big Innovation Centre's and Mayer's work, Blueprint for Better Business (2017) – another UK-based not-for-profit think-tank – implicitly takes as given the legislative framework within which companies operate. Instead, it puts forward five behavioural principles of what must be done for a company to be purpose-driven. They focus on key business relationships that must be acted on in an integrated manner.

Its framework starts with purpose:

- "... having purpose which delivers long-term sustainable performance for the economy: Operates true to purpose that serves society, respects the dignity of people and so generates a fair return to responsible investors. Enables and welcomes public scrutiny of the alignment between stated purpose and actual performance".

It then goes onto describe what it means to be purpose-led to live and to deliver it:

- "... being a responsible and responsive employer: Treats everyone with dignity and provides fair pay for all. Enables and welcomes constructive dialogue about its behaviour in keeping true to its purpose. Fosters innovation, leadership and personal accountability. Protects and nurtures all who work for it to ensure people also learn, contribute and thrive".
- "... being honest and fair with customers and suppliers: Seeks to build lasting relationships with customers and suppliers. Deals honestly with customers, providing good and safe products and services. Treats suppliers fairly, pays promptly what it owes and expects its suppliers to do the same. Openly shares its knowledge to enable customers and suppliers to make better informed choices".
- "... being a guardian of the environment for future generations: Honours its duty to protect the natural world and conserve finite resources. Contributes knowledge and experience to promote better regulation for the benefit of society as a whole rather than protecting self-interest. Invests in developing skills, knowledge and understanding in wider society to encourage informed citizenship".
- "... being a good citizen: Considers each person affected by the decisions as if he or she were a member of each decision-maker's own community. Seeks and provides access to opportunities for the less privileged people. Makes a full and fair contribution to society by structuring its business or operations to pay promptly all taxes that are properly due".

In Chapter 6, these five principles are drawn on as additional verification, again via benchmarking, of the proposed core business process model and its application to the case study company as a purpose-driven company. Again, the successful benchmarking is also used to demonstrate the wider applicability of the model to a wide array of companies and sectors.

Similar to Blueprint for Better Business, Edmans (2020) focuses primarily on actions at the individual company level for it to be purpose-driven. His starting point is to define a company's purpose. His proposition is that growing the pie highlights the power of purpose, and a company's reason for its being and the role it plays in the world focusing on the long term. He sees the need for a shift in mentality away from a zero-sum game on how to split the pie. Edmans demonstrates, through a comprehensive body of empirical evidence, that it is not a fixed pie requiring a trade-off between sacrificing profit for benefits to society; rather, it is a case of growing the pie. As he puts it, purpose is not at the expense of profits, and profits are not at the expense of purpose.

Edmans draws out general principles based on a large-scale research of companies across a wide variety of industries in different contexts. His recommendations on what to do concentrate on the company itself with a series of practical actions with respect to leaders' incentives in rewarding long-term performance; stewardship and engaged investors; shareholder activism and share re-purchasers; and the collective power of individuals.

Overall, a company's purpose is the jumping-off point for defining its values, which in turn collectively determine its culture, which then collectively drive its strategy, which – with successful execution – deliver its purpose, with profit being a natural outcome. Rather than Drucker's idea that 'culture eats strategy for breakfast', it is now the case that 'purpose eats strategy for breakfast'. As such, purpose for a company is a source of long-term sustainable competitive advantage.

To a great extent, much of what is proposed to date relates to setting out the much-needed guidance on what must be done for or what a company must do in order for it to be purpose-driven. Various proposed legislative changes and elements of differing programmes/initiatives will have differing traction in re-connecting business with society. Stakeholders, boards, chairpersons and CEOs are far from being a homogeneous group. Whatever legislative change is in effect and/or initiative(s) a company may decide to adopt, there remains the overriding challenge for CEOs to actually deliver their company's defined purpose.

What is now required is a core business process model to deliver the 'How'. As in life and so in business, it is not so much the 'What' is said and done, but the '*How*' it is said and done that yields the greatest impact on a company's people to deliver.

References

A Blueprint for Better Business (2017). *ibid.*
Edmans, A. (2020). *ibid.*
https://alexedmans.com/the-purposeful-company
Mayer, C. (2018). *ibid.*
The Big Innovation Centre (2016). *ibid.*

Chapter 4

THE '*HOW?*'

Implement the 'Heightened Integrity Model'

What is now needed from a CEO's perspective is an evidence-based business model derived from best practice for the '*How*' to deliver a company's defined purpose. It is the CEO who has the delegated executive authority, responsibility and accountability for delivering the board's endorsed purpose for the company. With the growing body of recommended policies of what should be put in place and what practices and actions a company should take to be a purpose-driven company, there still remains a big gap. The '*What*' has to be executed.

Whilst some progress has been achieved and the '*How*' has been taken seriously by several writers, there remains a lot of room for further work:

- Blueprint for Better Business's (2017) five principles provide a framework to guide decision-making in terms of defining purpose and the behaviours needed to build character and achieve purpose. It states that they are 'tools' for what sort of behaviour is expected of a purpose-driven company. It also sets out principles and proxies for how a company board can measure progress being made and how to focus on material matters to facilitate prioritisation. In being at the board level, there remains the need for the '*How*' a company realises its purpose in practice, and the '*How*' to use these invaluable tools in order to actually deliver the five principles in operational terms.
- Mayer's (2018) work predominantly encompasses the '*Why*' and the '*What*' of purpose. His focus is on making the case for company purpose that corporate control should reside with scarce capital which is no longer predominantly financial. And there is the need to balance and integrate the components of capital (i.e. human, intellectual, material, natural, social and financial capital). Whilst he recommends a raft of policy change in legislation to stimulate greater purposefulness in companies, he also recognises explicitly that law alone cannot force good conduct by companies. He also sees the need, for example, for trust and transparency for a company's defined purpose to be delivered.

- Edmans (2020) devotes the section of his book *How to Grow the Pie* to the perspective of the '*Enterprise*', '*Investors*' and '*Citizens*'. Much of the discussion in the chapter '*Enterprise*' is about attributes or principles that a purpose company should have; i.e. the '*What*' that must be done (e.g. excellence in delivery; that a purpose statement must be focused, selective and translate into action by being embedded in a company; and with an attitude of empowerment, investment in a company's people and rewarding them). For his '*communicating beyond purpose*' (under '*Enterprise*'), Edmans develops some of the '*How*' this might best be done by proposing that communication must be personal and must be two-way. The proposed core business process model expands on this specific element of the '*How*' considerably in Chapter 5.
- Whilst preferring the term 'moral leadership', the HOW Institute for Society (2020) – a US think-tank – has a very similar purpose-driven objective as The Big Innovation Centre and Blueprint for Better Business in the need to respond to the growing disconnect between business and society. Its moral leadership framework consists of let purpose lead; inspire and motivate others; be animated by values and virtues; and build moral muscle. In terms of the '*What*' to do to build moral muscle, its recommended moral leadership practices are start with a pause; see the humanity in everyone; foster freedom; act with courage; seek the truth; uphold ethical standards; and demonstrate humility.

As these works concentrate on the rationale and evidence for the '*Why*' and the '*What*', they do not seek to put forward a business model for the '*How*'. They do provide, however, the much-needed foundation for proceeding to the '*How*' to realise in practice a company's purpose.

Governance, Delivery and Performance

There are two pivotal relationships for the delivery of a company's defined purpose. One relates to governance in terms of the interaction between a company's chairperson and its CEO. For defining a company's purpose, most commonly it is an iterative process between a board, its chairperson, its CEO and its leadership team – with preferably significant involvement of their company's people – that results in an agreed definition. Thereafter, the company's board occupies the governance stewardship-trustee role of ensuring that the company's purpose is realised. It is the chairperson's role to monitor and review the CEO's performance for the successful execution of the company's purpose; as is the case, for example, with a company's strategy.

The other critical relationship is the interaction between middle management and their company's people, which is about the reality of delivery. It is here that execution of a company's purpose must be alive. It is the daily delivery of a host of individual decisions and actions that result in the realisation of company's purpose. This is all about a company's culture. That is, how a company's leaders and its people interact daily and their mindsets; which, in turn, drives behaviour and performance; and, hence, the successful execution of the company's defined purpose in practical terms.

There is no single blockbuster action or initiative that results in delivery. It is the relentless consistency of message and required behaviours that delivers. Middle management, as well as the CEO and the senior leadership team, must be completely behind the agreed purpose. It cannot be simply cascaded down. It must be interactive with radical engagement and two-way communication between leaders – importantly, at all levels – and a company's people.

With respect to business performance, a landmark assessment of the impact of the interaction between leaders and a company's people and its financial performance is by Edmans (2012):

- He conducts a rigorous longitudinal statistical analysis of the changes in the stock value of companies listed in the Great Place to Work Institute's annual survey, '100 Best Companies to Work for America in America': 'Overall workplace quality' is defined in terms of the culture set by management and employees' views of their corporation, their own job and the interaction with the culture set by management.
- This is where the company's culture is defined in terms of attributes such as listening, speaking, thinking, caring and celebrating; and, where employees have a very high level of trust in their company and its leaders in terms of credibility, respect, fairness, pride and camaraderie.

He demonstrates that there is a direct causal link between firms' financial performance and overall workplace quality, as measured by the Great Place to Work Institute's survey:

- His analysis shows that the top 100 companies generate 2.3 per cent to 3.8 per cent higher stock return per year than their peers over a 28-year period, which when compounded is 89 per cent to 184 per cent.
- To be in the top 100 companies, companies have to achieve the highest 'workplace quality score'. This is derived from two

propriety surveys: employees' response to the Trust Index survey and management's response to the Cultural Audit survey.
- He concludes that overall workplace quality probably only matters when it reaches very high levels and this results in increased stock value, and that there is little difference for company value between low and moderate workplace practice.

A complementary study by Guiso, Sapienza and Zingales (2015) to that of Edmans – also based on the results of Great Place to Work Institute's work – confirms his main findings. It goes further and adds that high levels of perceived integrity are positively correlated with higher productivity, better industrial relations and higher levels of attractiveness to prospective job applicants.

Several comprehensive literature reviews (i.e. The Big Innovation Centre 2016; A Blueprint for Better Business 2017; Mayer 2018; Edmans 2020) also provide a substantial body of evidence that collectively concludes that purpose companies outperform their peers in financial terms.

A purpose-defined company's characteristics include many of the attributes of the high-performing companies ranked as top 100 companies by the Great Place to Work Institute:

- This is where a company's culture and employees' trust positively interact. There is a higher level of integrity and interaction in the company between its leaders and its people resulting in higher level performance in delivering its goal.
- Employees have greater self-worth, fulfilment, higher levels of job satisfaction and feel empowered, as is required in a purpose-defined company.

Heightened Integrity: The Hub of the Model

'Heightened integrity' is defined as when a company's leaders and its people proactively interact and operate transparently with the highest levels of ethical values and behaviour in the execution of their company's goal: its defined purpose.

Heightened integrity is the hub of the proposed business model.

The term 'heightened integrity' is employed because it is imperative that CEOs lead their company on the front foot in a proactive, bold and consistent manner (and not in a passive way) on a higher ethical plane. When these attributes are fully operational, they result in a company's leaders and its people delivering exceptional overall workplace quality and superior business performance, and hence its defined purpose. They lead to greater business success as well as moral satisfaction.

The definition of integrity must go beyond broad generalities which include various aspects of wholeness, soundness, honesty, transparency, trust, values and so on. They tend to be passive responsive concepts. Integrity is an intangible asset. Integrity cannot be practised in the passive or responsive manner by a CEO when leading a company and interacting with its people. That would be insufficient to deliver a company's purpose.

The modus operandi of a purpose-driven company, or how it operates to implement its defined purpose, can be characterised in terms of the following:

- Its purpose flows throughout and is embedded in the whole fabric of the company from the board to the shop-floor, covering the practicalities of its governance, culture, commercial strategy, management, structure, systems and daily operations; it pervades its whole supply chain and all its customer sets; and it goes beyond formal announcements.
- Its value proposition; its set of values and beliefs; its living conducive culture; and its goals and strategies.
- Its leaders and the company's people interact with integrity and high visibility; it operates and is seen to operate on a high ethical plane; a proactive stance is taken as to what is acceptable and unacceptable vis-à-vis the company's defined purpose; and all of its affairs are conducted with integrity.

The proposition is that CEOs deliver bigger benefits for society and bigger financial value for their business over the long term and in a sustainable manner when they lead and operate their purpose-defined company with heightened integrity:

- The challenge for CEOs is to lead and operate with integrity so that it ratchets up the company's performance to the much higher level that is required to deliver its defined purpose. It is a prerequisite, not an afterthought.
- It places obligations on a company's leaders to create a culture that positively impacts on its people so that they reciprocate and take – and are given by the company's leaders – the authority, responsibility and accountability for the actual delivery of the company's defined purpose. People, generally, want to work for and do business with people they trust, and avoid those they do not trust.
- There is greater visibility in what a company's leaders and its people say and in what they do, and how they behave.

The 'Heightened Integrity Model'

The proposed business model is actually a core business process model. A company's business model encompasses, for example, how it defines its value proposition, customer sets, products/services to be sold, key business processes and resource allocation. This then forms the framework for structuring its costs and revenue streams to deliver its objective and profits. A summary of the Group's business model is provided in the Appendix.

A core business process is a sub-model that is an integral part of a company's business model. A core business process model is made up of the minimum individual but interrelated tasks or subprocesses that accomplish a defined organisational goal of value creation (i.e. its purpose). It encompasses the entire organisation and impacts all of its activities. It harmonises implementation of the management intangibles that are required for the actualisation of a company's purpose. When successfully embedded, it then becomes a core competence of the company. That is, heightened integrity is the engine for the execution and delivery of the company's previously defined purpose.

The 'Heightened Integrity Model', when successfully implemented by CEOs, is the core process that delivers a company's overall business model for the execution of its purpose, values, culture and strategy.

The proposed model has six interrelated subprocesses (see Figure 4.1). The dynamics of these subprocesses, or how they fit together, are that the first three subprocesses provide the required 'enabling platform' for the subsequent three 'delivery' subprocesses. Whilst there is a logical sequence to the six subprocesses, they are interdependent and must be implemented in a mutually reinforcing manner. They are not stand-alone activities or initiatives.

The innovative model is based predominantly on the author's CEO experience of leading what became a purpose company, a mid-cap multinational corporation in the chemical engineering sector, and prior senior executive experience under very different ownership structures, as a director of a FTSE/NYSE listed company and as a partner of a Big 4 accounting firm.

Purpose statement subprocess: The words of the purpose statement must be big, bold, ambitious, authentic, inspirational and practical. It must be readily understood at all levels of the company. A company's purpose statement has to be aspirational and motivational for its people, and more. It has to authentically respond to the question of what does the company actually give to society to make it better in practical terms (Blueprint for Better Business 2020). It must meet a real societal need that the company's people can identify with and value. It must positively inspire, invigorate and energise a company's people. Employees

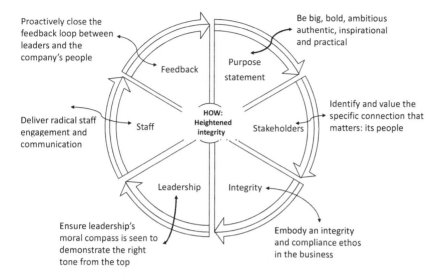

Figure 4.1 The 'Heightened Integrity Model'.

are not driven in their daily working life by wishing to maximise shareholder profits.

Stakeholders subprocess: Identify and value the one that matters – its people. There is a plethora of stakeholders for most companies, ranging from shareholders, board members, employees, customers, suppliers, trade unions, media, regulators, non-governmental agencies to government. Each can occupy a different role and have a different relative importance or materiality in a company's affairs and success. The challenge is to identify and value the one that is highly material in terms of impact and influence. Whilst a company's board (led by its chairperson) defines, adopts and is the trustee of its purpose, it is a company's people who actually deliver its performance and hence its purpose in operational terms. Consequently, there is a need to galvanise a company's people around its purpose. A company's people are the specific connection that matters for the operational delivery of its previously defined purpose.

Integrity/Compliance subprocess: Embody an integrity and compliance ethos in the business. Many leaders promulgate the need for their business to act with integrity. Much of this, however, is compliance driven and can often be a 'box ticking' exercise. The alignment of a company's people with its purpose has to go beyond compliance of what not to do. There has to be proactive promotion of engendering good or otherwise the company's purpose will not be realised. 'Embody' is the keyword whereby the ethos becomes part of the way of doing business, both internally and externally. This calls for employees themselves taking responsibility for what is acceptable and unacceptable behaviour and performance with respect to actual implementation of their company's stated purpose. For leaders, there is the attendant benefit of spending less time and fewer resources checking that compliance matters are fulfilled, with resultant increases in productivity.

Leadership subprocess: Ensure leader's moral compass is seen to demonstrate the right tone from the top. Demonstrated tone from the top is more than leadership having a moral compass or stating a North Star. What matters is employees' perception of a leader's trust, worthiness and demonstration (i.e. what they do) of their ethical values and not their proclaimed values (i.e. what they say). The company's moral compass has to be seen to be demonstrated from the top by the CEO. The impact on employees of how a CEO responds to compliance and especially integrity issues sets the ethical benchmark of what is acceptable and unacceptable for the realisation of the company's defined purpose.

Staff subprocess: Deliver radical staff engagement and communication. Staff perception is shaped by what and how their leaders communicate and interact with them. There is the vital need to ensure that employees decode communications and the way it is intended with respect to the company's purpose, and that leaders receive feedback contributions in return. It culminates in enlightened empowerment of a company's people by its leaders. In turn, when a company empowers its people, it enters a virtuous circle of deeper staff commitment, greater loyalty and increased performance (e.g. higher productivity, product innovation, superior customer service, larger revenues and profits) and delivery of its defined purpose.

Feedback subprocess: Proactively close the feedback loop between leaders and the company's people. This is the imperative for the successful implementation of the core business process model and subsequently the actual realisation of the company's previously defined purpose. Companies have a considerable range of processes for communicating between its leaders and its people, many of which are under the control of management. There is the need to adopt a system whereby the feedback process is independent of management and totally transparent to all staff. It requires autonomy, transparency and informed feedback and generates user loyalty with a right of reply through a positive feedback loop. Employees have to be truly empowered to feedback issues that could compromise delivery of their company's purpose. The acid test here is the extent to which a company's people will ask, and continue to ask, their leaders challenging questions – which require cogent replies publicly.

All six subprocesses have to be implemented with heightened integrity. Leading and operating a company with heightened integrity is the hub of the core business process model. It thereby ensures that the company's purpose courses throughout the whole organisation and all of its various actions. Leading and operating a company with heightened integrity embeds purpose-led thinking into all areas of a business. This is how the modus operandi of the 'How' is delivered.

References

A Blueprint for Better Business (2017). *ibid.*
A Blueprint for Better Business (2020). *"Purpose for PLCs: Time for boards to focus"*. A Blueprint for Better Business. London.
Edmans, A. (2012). *ibid.*
Edmans, A. (2020). *ibid.*
Guiso, L., Sapienza, P. and Zingales, L. (2015). *"The value of corporate culture booth school of business"*. The University of Chicago, Chicago.
Mayer, C (2018). *ibid.*
The HOW Institute for Society (2020). *"The State of Moral Leadership"*. The HOW Institute for Society. New York.

Chapter 5

DEMONSTRATION

Application of the Model to
the Case Study Multinational
Corporation

The Case Study Corporation

By leading and operating the case study corporation with heightened integrity, it is transformed from a 'dog' to being a recognised world leader.

The case study corporation, Hamworthy Combustion Group (the Group), operates in one of the largest, most dynamic markets in the world: global, environmental, downstream oil and gas. The Group designs, manufactures, commissions and services large-scale combustion burners for a variety of generally noxious industry end-user customers in downstream oil and gas (e.g. flares, petrochemical processing plants and the marine sector) and hot water and steam raising applications (e.g. industrial, power plants and marine sector).

The results from the case study multinational corporation cover the seven-year period from when the new CEO is appointed by its new owners, a private equity house, to when the Group is subsequently sold.

The new CEO's remit is to grow the Group and its profits. However, the Group is in decline with profits in the year prior to his appointment having fallen in a growing market. It suffers from underinvestment and has a highly dysfunctional blame culture. There is a lot of inertia, with it being a long-established company and limping along in a state of disrepair. The Group has no clear strategy or coherent business plan for its 13 companies located in 12 countries with a total of 16 offices. Whilst the Group also has a highly dysfunctional culture, the new CEO sees a number of core management control processes that assist greatly in delivering its future success. In conversations with colleagues at all levels, the CEO describes them as 'golden nuggets' to be polished and enhanced.

The new CEO establishes an invigorated like-minded executive team. It consists of two incumbent directors plus an internally promoted director and three external director appointments along with the established leaders of the larger country offices of France, Italy and the US – so as not to be UK-centric. Box 5.1 provides an overview of the CEO's modus operandi.

By year seven, the Group is transformed; from a 'dog' to being a recognised world leader. Customers acknowledge it as providing world-leading products and services from its expanded global network of 20 companies located in 19 countries with a total of 24 offices; thereby encompassing 80 per cent of world Gross Domestic Product. The transformation is due to its committed executive team and leaders at all levels operating with heightened integrity throughout the Group, thereby realising its defined purpose and consequently its superior profitability.

Box 5.1 About the CEO...

- He is appointed as CEO by the private equity owners due to his considerable senior executive international experience and a track record of business success along with the attendant 'scars-on-the-back'.
- The CEO recognises that the job is highly challenging:
  - The multinational corporation is declining; it is in the doldrums; it suffers from little investment; and its culture is highly dysfunctional.
  - He is not an engineer and has little technical credibility. And, the Group's people expect cost-cutting and redundancies from the new CEO brought in by its new owners, a private equity house.
- The CEO's personal style is shaped by his views that:
  - Companies and individuals should give something back to society and thereby contribute to the betterment of society.
  - A company's people do not turn up for work with the objective of maximising shareholder value. They want purpose to their job with self-worth and fulfilment from it.
  - He must 'walk-the-walk' and be seen to be so doing, not 'talk the talk'.
- He sees his immediate priority is to secure significant investment in new substantial R&D facilities, thereby
  - Testing that the private equity house owner is actually committed to investing in the Group.
  - Providing the much-needed physical infrastructure for the definition and launch of world-leading, technically and operationally, combustion burners.
  - Demonstrating very early to the Group's people tangible success.

    The investment case for a major new combustion test rig is approved by the Board within 12 weeks of the CEO joining.

- Recognising that the agenda he faces is huge, the CEO
  - Proceeds in 'a radical, incremental evolutionary manner'.
  - Senses that the best way of securing real traction at all levels in the Group is to get bits and pieces of actual progress achieved in different parts of the Group's activities and its international network of companies (often at different paces).
  - Does not define and launch a corporate transformation programme nor a culture change programme.
  - Holds as his North Star the Group's purpose. Its definition is rolled out in an almost self-revealing manner rather than being proselytised and cascaded from the top-down.

This chapter demonstrates how the core business process model can be applied to a company. The 'enabling subprocesses' section largely summarises what has to be changed and put in place in the Group and hence what subsequently has to be achieved by the 'delivery subprocesses'.

Further demonstration of application of the 'Heightened Integrity Model' to the Group to realise its defined purpose is set out in the subsequent chapter 'Verification' (Chapter 6). The Group's practices and experience of what it does are benchmarked against third-party best practice. This provides verification of the core business process model and its demonstrated application to the case study company, and its rigor in having wider applicability to companies in all sectors.

The case study provides a considerable amount of information presented in a frank manner. A lot of commercially sensitive company data are set out which are not usually seen in case studies. On being sold by its private sector owners, the Group is subsumed into a much larger corporate group and is likewise effectively disbanded. And its former owners, a private equity company, is likewise subsumed into a much larger financial institution and is effectively disbanded.

Enabling Subprocesses

Purpose Statement: Be Big, Bold, Ambitious, Authentic, Inspirational and Practical

People generally do not turn up for work thinking, "*I'm going to increase shareholder value today*". They want an emotional connection, self-worth, meaning, personal development and fulfilment from their work.

As indicated, the Group is a 'dog' – drifting, underinvested and with declining profits in a growing market with no vision or stated purpose other than for it to be as profitable as possible. With a new CEO and executive team, the Group's purpose is defined in terms of why it exists and what it does, as summarised in Box 5.2. Its bold purpose sets out its value proposition in terms of business materiality and in a practical manner that is meaningful, authentic and inspirational to its people as well as being highly ambitious.

Box 5.2 The Group's Purpose

We contribute to a healthier environment for society and become a guardian of the environment for future generations.

We benefit society with products and services that result in cleaner air and reduced depletion of natural resources in a long-term sustainable manner.

We provide technical solutions for reducing the adverse environmental impact of companies operating predominantly in the global, dynamic and generally noxious downstream oil and gas sectors.

We deliver world-leading, cost-effective combustion burners and related services to reduce emissions and increase fuel efficiency with absolute safety for

- Downstream oil and gas companies in the flares, petro-chemicals and the marine sector.
- Hot water and steam raising applications in the industrial, agriculture/food processing, power plants and the marine sectors.

This focused and actionable purpose explains to employees how the Group meets a societal need in providing some resolution to global environmental challenges as well as growing the business, thereby contributing to the long-term sustainable performance of the Group and the economy. This purpose, along with a newly formulated motivational vision of being a world leader through product technical excellence and cost reduction, is accompanied by an ambitious strategy for doubling the size of the Group within five years, with profits growing faster than revenue.

The Group's purpose provides a disciplined strategic direction and subsequently a quantified milestone for its long-term aspiration. Its innovative focus is necessarily on R&D activities so as to specify and deliver world-leading product performance for emission reduction, greater fuel efficiency and absolute safety for its products (i.e. combustion burners).

Box 5.3 Purpose and Profitability Trade-off at a Point of a Major Decision

After several years, when the Group's business performance is now turned around and it is highly successful with commensurate profitability, the private equity owners decide to prepare the Group to be taken to market for sale. This is during the annual round of business planning and budget formulation.

The private equity owners propose adoption of a highly ambitious growth in profits for the subsequent three-year term. This would compromise the delivery of the Group's purpose. Such an ambitious level of profitability could only be achieved by reducing the recruitment of additional service engineers and reducing other operating costs expenditure. The additional service engineers are required to ensure that the Group's combustion burner products perform optimally at customer installations for longer term and sustainable reduction of emissions and increased fuel efficiency with absolute safety.

The rapport between the private equity owners and the Group's leadership team is sufficiently strong for the proposal to be aborted. The argument from the Group's leadership team is in terms that the private equity owners readily appreciate. That is, such a highly ambitious profit target would be the private equity firm's own target unilaterally imposed on the Group. It would not be owned (analytically or emotionally) by the Group's leadership team and hence it was highly unlikely that it would be achieved.

This also facilitates focused engagement with suppliers and customers by setting out the strategic intent of the company in terms that they can readily relate to. It drives priorities in resource allocation and the primacy of R&D for world-leading product performance with excellent after-sales service, thereby serving the needs of clients and society.

The Group's purpose and vision motivates and inspires its people. It responds to them wanting greater fulfilment and self-worth from their work, and working with a Group that they can be proud of as it contributes to society through its products and services directly resulting in a healthier environment.

However, there are challenges of delivering the Group's purpose, which can involve trade-offs at the point of major decisions. One example is when the Group's private equity owners are preparing the Group for sale during the annual business plan and budget setting process, as summarised in Box 5.3. A shorter-term, higher-profitability budget is proposed by the owners for a three-year forecast term. This is at the cost of investment in customer services and hence the operational performance of the Group's products at client sites, with an adverse impact on delivery of its purpose.

Making trade-offs are a normal aspect of corporate life, as seen, for example, in deciding the balance between investing for the shorter term and for the longer term. For a purpose-defined company, the number and range of potential trade-offs increase and are more complex than for a company with the objective of maximising shareholder returns, due to the former's greater variety and larger number of stakeholders.

Consequently, it is important that there is a balanced set of non-financial and financial metrics for a company's board to measure the success of its CEO's execution of its purpose. A set of non-financial and financial metrics is proposed in Chapter 6 which seek to encompass the behavioural engagement and operational aspects of a purpose-driven company. It must be recognised, however, that it is impossible for any one set of performance metrics to meet all the nuances of the differences in the specific values, moral philosophy and, hence, requirements of all of the various stakeholders of a purpose-driven company.

Stakeholders: Identify and Value the Specific One That Matters - Its People

With the purpose of a company being defined and signed off by its board, there is the need to identify and value the specific connections that matter for the actual delivery of the defined purpose. Here, the most critical stakeholder is a company's people. It is the company's employees who deliver its performance and purpose. This strongly resonates with Blueprint for Better Business's treating each person as a someone, not a something.

For the Group, much work is needed in terms of how it treats its people. The prior leadership style and culture is largely command and control, and hierarchical and secretive. It has a highly dysfunctional culture. Its people have a feeling of alienation, detachment and disengagement. There is little trust in management, employee morale is poor and staff turnover is significantly higher than its industry average.

Symptomatic of this adverse state of affairs is that staff terms and conditions are highly inconsistent and its 'human resource' (HR) services is essentially an inadequate administrative payroll system.

A required starting point to show that its people are valued is to put in place, as a minimum, a blue-chip hygiene range of staff terms and conditions. As a result of recruiting towards the end of year one a first-rate Human Resources Director, staff terms and conditions of employment are transformed by early year three (Table 5.1).

Table 5.1 Transformation of staff terms and conditions

Year 1	Year 3: Blue-chip, hygiene
Administration Payroll function No data: • Number of employees by office • Number of employees by main function (Sales, Operations, Spares and Service, Finance, HR, IT) • Number of employees by length of service	Performance appraisals Communication programme Standardised contracts Pension advice Training records Occupational health Joiners induction Car scheme Staff handbook Company sick pay Absence monitoring Flexible retirement/part- Exit/leavers interviews time working Joining instructions Payroll system Recruitment tracking Personnel records Salary regrading/alignment Loyalty recognition Terms and conditions Training programmes Disciplinary processes Commercial/management Incentivised salary reviews Staff satisfaction surveys Apprenticeship programme Lunch and Learn sessions

In addition, three specific initiatives are also put in place by the Group:

• Early in year one, the Group introduces an apprenticeship programme, which subsequently attains university degree certification. In contrast to many conventional apprentice programmes, whereby all apprentices are paid the same in their training years, high-flyer performers are rewarded for their success with higher remuneration and are given more challenging work opportunities. The apprenticeship programme exceeds all expectations. It sends a clear positive emotional message to all staff – in both the UK and throughout its international network of country offices – that the Group is investing in the business for the future, even though the Group is to be sold at a point in time, and that its people are being developed for the future irrespective of who might own the Group.

- Later in year one, the Group retains a highly qualified nurse to visit staff when they are absent from work due to illness to ensure that they receive the appropriate medical support. This is particularly important for many of the Group's people who travel a lot internationally on business and often have to operate under arduous remote on-site conditions.
- Early in year three, at the suggestion of staff, a four-and-a-half-day working week is introduced with the normal working week finishing at mid-day on the Friday. The total number of hours worked per week remains the same, by lengthening the working day.

They all also make sound commercial sense: The apprenticeship programme provides the combustion specialists of the future; the medical support reduces absenteeism and hence results in increase in productivity; and the four-and-a half-day working week is attractive for recruiting new staff. Collectively, they assist in underpinning the commercial delivery of the Group's purpose.

The Group's people most positively recognise that a transformation in how they are viewed and treated is in place, which go beyond contractual matters. Its people appreciate that they are now employed in a professional manner with a positive relationship being enjoyed between them and their employer. They are increasingly being treated with dignity and are valued.

Integrity/Compliance: Embody an Integrity and Compliance Ethos in the Business

A compliance-driven business is insufficient to deliver a company's purpose. It has to go beyond the 'not do bad'. It has to promote the 'do good'. There is a need to embody an integrity-driven ethos in a company, one of operating at a higher ethical plane.

With an integrity-driven regime, compliance in a company becomes an outcome without it being an objective. Moreover, ethics (knowing what to do), competence (having the ability to do it) and accountability (people taking responsibility to do it) are necessary individually but are not sufficient. They have to be aligned collectively so that staff themselves take responsibility for what is acceptable and unacceptable behaviour and 'do good' and not 'do bad', thereby resulting in accountability building in a company from the bottom-up.

A commonality of many codes of ethics or conduct is that they are compliance- and governance-driven and can be a 'box-ticking' exercise. In many respects, they contain a number of 'motherhood and apple pie' statements in that the majority of employees would not disagree that they should support them. In addition to often being a comprehensive and a long list of items, which many employees would have difficulty remembering, it is questionable whether exhortation-type statements would result in embodying an ethos in a company that would be motivational to staff and result in a positive impact on behaviour and business performance.

For embodying an integrity/compliance ethos in a company, the starting point is one of assuming that all its people act with integrity and that none would deliberately put the company at risk. And, if staff were to act in a corrupt or illegal manner, then this would over time become evident and the appropriate corrective action would be taken decisively.

Additionally, with staff being empowered to make decisions, there is always the case that on occasions a wrong decision is made. Consequently, if a wrong decision is made, then the individual involved should feel empowered to raise this and seek assistance to resolve it. There has to be an ethos that it is a greater sin not to raise the result of the wrong decision and try to sort it out than making the wrong decision itself. Here a company's people would be taking responsibility and would be empowered to make decisions and control resources that directly influence the actions of others and as a consequence ensure that the company's purpose would be delivered.

There is a need for a code of values that go beyond generalities and are specific to the individual company if the desire is for it to have a direct impact on the preferred type of behaviour from its people.

The Group's former management's regime is compliance- and risk averse–driven. There is an atmosphere of little trust with there often being secret 'side deals' between managers. Board meetings are orchestrated by the former incumbent CEO. Overall, there is inconsistent moral fibre displayed by leaders in the Group, thereby providing a poor role model for its people. To address this, the new CEO and executive team seek to emphasise 'how things are done around here' in an open and transparent manner. It thereby provides a role model from the top for employees as to how they are now expected to engage with their Group and their people.

By early year three, the Group's leadership team believes it is timely to define a simple and an easily communicated set of 'values' or 'ethics' that can be adopted by management and staff at all levels. By this time, traction has been achieved in changing the company's culture from being a highly negative one to one being much more open and positive with greater trust and transparency between its leaders and its people.

The view is taken by the leadership team that the set of Values should:

- Be directive, so as to bring about a distinct and common set of behaviours for individuals and groups of individuals.

- Have resonance with staff, by being specific and meaningful to them in the practicalities of their working day.
- Be limited in number, clear and simple, and thereby readily understood across the multilingual, multinational company.

Following considerable discussion by the leadership team and pilot airing of the concepts and their definitions in a variety of forums, the following code of values is adopted:

- Treat colleagues, suppliers and customers like you want to be treated.
- No surprises: communicate proactively.
- No negative emails. Discuss: speak directly or phone.
- Keep within delegated authority or consult upwards: Scheme of Delegated Authority.

The set of values are promulgated in a low-key rather than in an evangelical manner. The leadership team believes that this is preferable to having a self-standing programme or a top-down culture change integrity or ethics programme.

Table 5.2 provides the rationale in the code of values in terms of how they result in a preferred behaviour that will reinforce a positive and constructive performance-driven culture by staff. That is, the code of values also provides practical reasons as to why the Group's people should adopt them.

Table 5.2 Rationale of the code of values

Code	Rationale
'Treat colleagues, suppliers and customers like you want to be treated'	For the individual, this provides a personal benchmark as to what is acceptable and unacceptable behaviour. The logic of the ordering of colleagues, then suppliers and then customers is that if colleagues are treated well, then such behaviour would be apparent to suppliers. Suppliers were put before customers, as the Group outsourced some 80 per cent by cost of products sold. And, if suppliers were being treated well, then there was a higher probability that customers were also being treated well.
'No surprises: communicate proactively'	As there was a culture of wanting staff to take responsibility and make decisions, it was recognised that honest mistakes would be made. If mistakes were made, then staff should report them early so that they could be resolved quickly.

(Continued)

Code	Rationale
'No negative emails. Discuss: speak directly or phone'	With a global marketplace and with 23 offices in 19 countries in different time zones, email communication was vital. However, with staff operating in around a dozen different native languages, email correspondence could become tortuous and easily misunderstood. Staff were encouraged when issues needed to be sorted out to speak directly rather than engage in what often could become an iteration of increasingly negative email exchanges.
'Keep within delegated authority or consult upwards': Scheme of Delegated Authority	This primarily related to the financial limits of approval of staff in various roles (and for certain departments, the level of technical risk of contracts). If staff felt they needed to exceed their delegated limits, then they were encouraged to consult a more senior colleague and then to make the appropriate decision. On all known occasions when staff followed this process, they subsequently made the decision.

Applied in isolation, an integrity and compliance ethos can be disjointed and fragmented within the overall organisation. To shift from a compliance-based management programme to a heightened integrity-driven business requires leadership's moral compass to demonstrate the right tone from the top. This is seen most clearly by how a CEO handles compliance and integrity issues.

Delivery Subprocesses

Leadership: Ensure Leadership's Moral Compass Is Seen to Demonstrate the Right Tone from the Top

The key and challenging words in the core business process model's '*Ensure that leader's moral compass is seen to demonstrate the right moral tone from the top*' are '*is seen to demonstrate*'. Proclaimed values of leaders are not important to staff. What is important is employees' perception of leaders. A CEO's behaviour and decisions can be judged in terms of whether it is in self-interest or with the best of values. There is the need not only to set out what employees should not do but also to encourage them to do good. It must have a sharp edge in terms of making hard decisions based on setting the pace for high performance whilst at the same time operating transparently with the highest levels of ethical behaviour, i.e. heightened integrity.

CEOs must '*walk the talk*' and be seen to do so. This can be illustrated in terms of how CEOs handle integrity and compliance issues, and whether they are reactive or proactive to them, with the ensuing differential impact on a company's people. For example, where a CEO is seen to be reactive to a compliance issue, then the impact on employees would be negligible: That is how they would expect their CEO to react. On the other hand, when a CEO is seen to be proactive to an integrity issue, then the impact on employees could be very high. Consequently, the relative impact on employees of a CEO's resolution of issues thus ranges from negligible for reactive compliance, low for proactive compliance, medium for reactive integrity, to high for proactive integrity in handling issues. This provides a company's people with confidence in its leadership and consistency as to how issues are handled.

The following examples of the CEO's response to situations faced illustrate how the CEO demonstrates, and is seen to demonstrate, the right moral tone from the top (Boxes 5.4a–h):

- A reactive compliance decision by the CEO to an issue and hence having *negligible* impact on the Group's people, Boxes 5.4a and b.
- A proactive compliance decision by the CEO to an issue and hence having *low* impact on the Group's people, Boxes 5.4c and d.
- A reactive integrity decision by the CEO to an issue and hence having *medium* impact on the Group's people, Boxes 5.4e and f.
- A proactive integrity decision by the CEO to an issue and hence having *high* impact on the Group's people, Boxes 5.4g and h.

For the Group, the impact on its people of how its CEO responds to compliance and integrity issues become very clear. They witness the CEO's response to individual compliance and integrity issues and how decisions are made. Over time, and in marked contrast to the former regime, executives, managers and their people grow in confidence that issues and mistakes can and should be raised. It is also due to how the CEO responds to issues and mistakes raised by individual executives in meetings, where the reaction from the CEO is typically "*How do we resolve this collectively?*". As a consequence, the CEO is seen to be taking and demonstrating the moral high ground in terms of what is acceptable and unacceptable behaviour; he sets and is seen to demonstrate the Group's North Star.

Box 5.4a Integrity-Building   Approach: Reactive Compliance Decision

- *Situation*: Within two months of joining, the CEO is informed that the Group has entered an agreement with an Indian party for it to purchase the Intellectual Property Rights (IPR) of a vintage product in return for a royalty payment. However, the Indian government has not approved payment of the royalty. But, there is a circuitous route whereby payment could be made.

- *Response*: The CEO cancels the agreement. At best, the circuitous route is not ethical as it is avoiding a government ruling; at worst, it could be a corrupt practice in evading a legal requirement.
- Subsequently, however, the Japanese client requests that Group should test its own product's performance against that of the Japanese competitor's newly released equivalent product at the Group's R&D centre, with staff from the competitor being present. It is agreed amicably that this testing would proceed but without the presence of staff from the Japanese competitor, on the basis that they would gain highly commercial proprietary information on the Group's R&D facilities and test processes. This is accepted by the client. The Group's product clearly outperforms that of the Japanese competitor. The Japanese client continues to buy from the Group.

Impact on its people: Negligible.

Box 5.4b Integrity-Building Approach: Reactive Compliance Decision

- *Situation*: Within six months of joining, the CEO is informed by an executive that it might be useful for him to meet the CEO of a competitor firm for lunch in order to exchange views on market prospects and pricing.
- *Response*: The CEO does not arrange a meeting, and let it be known in a low-key but precise manner. Such a meeting could be open to interpretation as collusive behaviour in price fixing and hence would, in practice, be corrupt as it is breaking the law.

Impact on its people: Negligible.

It is noted in Chapter 4 that there are two pivotal relationships for the actual implementation of a company's purpose:

- The interaction between the chairperson and the CEO in terms of monitoring and reviewing the CEO's execution.

Box 5.4c Integrity-Building Approach: Proactive Compliance Decision

- *Situation*: The Group's Italian operation wants to source product from the Group's US operation and then integrate it into a much larger contract which is to be supplied to Iran. This is not prohibited by Italian law. However, the US government is increasing its scope of legislation against selling products to Iran, and the head of the Group's US firm brings this to the CEO's attention. Legal advice is taken. It confirms that selling the product as proposed is not currently breaking the US law but that under prospective legislation it would be illegal.
- *Response*: The decision is taken not to supply the US operation's product to the Italian operation for on-sale to Iran, even though currently it is not illegal to so do. The CEO's rationale is that the Group will act within the spirit of the law and not avoid it.

Impact on its people: Low.

Box 5.4d Integrity-Building Approach: Proactive Compliance Decision

- *Situation*: A long-serving and very experienced manager goes outside his delegated authority in submitting a quotation which he classifies as both high technical and high financial risk. His executive director asks the CEO what he should do about it.
- *Response*: The CEO requests the manager to meet him and asks him what he thought would happen if he did it again. The reply from the manager is 'You'll probably sack me'. The CEO also asks the manager what he felt the CEO is going to do immediately. The manager answered 'nothing'. The CEO tells the manager that he is correct on both accounts and that is the end of the meeting. (The manager continued to have a very successful career with the Group.) Both parties recognise what is appropriate behaviour in resolving an incident that could have led to dismissal of a member of staff who put the Group at a multi-million-pound risk through breaching, in a substantive and high-risk manner, the Scheme of Delegated Authority (counter to a major Group value).

Impact on its people: Low.

Box 5.4e Integrity-Building Approach: Reactive Integrity Decision

- *Situation*: A major Japanese customer has integrated into its installation the product of a Japanese competitor as a substitute for the Group's original equipment. The competitor's product looks in parts very similar to the Group's product. On examining the website and technical journals of the competitor, it is clear that the Japanese competitor infringes the Group's patented Intellectual Property Rights (IPR).
- *Response*: A senior executive goes to visit the Japanese customer. He explains that it was very embarrassing for him to report that they are purchasing and using a counterfeit product that infringes the Group's patented IPR. And, if the Japanese customer's product fails at its customer's installation, then they will not have insurance cover due to this infringement. The Japanese customer returns to buying the product from the Group and not from the Japanese competitor.

Impact on its people: Medium.

Box 5.4f Integrity-Building Approach: Reactive Integrity Decision

- *Situation*: At a UK factory workshop, a sometimes-troublesome trade union shop steward is noted as having 'fallen asleep' in the session. His manager instigates a disciplinary process on the grounds that falling asleep is a health and safety issue. The HR executive director advises the manager that this is inappropriate. The manager's response is that he was following the policies in the Group's staff handbook and if he withdraws the case then his authority will be undermined.
- *Response*: The HR executive director informs the manager that there will be a recommendation to cancel the process. The manager responds according to the staff handbook that such course of action is subject to appeal and that this should be heard with the attendance of another executive director. The executive team agrees to cancel the disciplinary process and informs the manager accordingly. It is evident that the manager cannot be trusted to act in a reasonable manner, so the decision is taken away from him. He also realises that he does not fit the Group's way of doing things and shortly leaves of his own accord.

Impact on its people: Medium.

Box 5.4g Integrity-Building Approach: Proactive Integrity Decision

- *Situation*: For the China country operation to be 100 per cent foreign-owned and to be able to import, trade locally and export, the Group is required to deposit in a local bank account a full year's operating costs. The signatories to the bank account are the local country manager and deputy. They have been promoted after the lack of success with a succession of two expatriate country managers.
- *Response*: In the course of a normal country office visit by the CEO, and over an informal dinner with all local staff, he is told in halting English by a junior staff member that the country manager has informed all the team that they have a personal responsibility to ensure that the China country office is highly profitable because of the trust that has been placed in them by the Group in depositing such a large amount of money locally under the direct control of the country management. Consequently, increasing trust in local management leads directly to local ownership of the drive to deliver improved business performance.

Impact on its people: High.

Box 5.4h Integrity-Building Approach: Proactive Integrity Decision

- *Situation*: In year four, with significant investment in a training centre, it is decided to appoint an experienced training manager for internal and client training. The training is delivered by full-time operational staff (who have been trained as trainers) on a volunteer basis in addition to their 'day job'. Whilst appearing to deliver very satisfactorily, the newly appointed training centre manager's style is 'command and control', which is counter to how the senior staff volunteer to conduct training. Despite several feedback sessions with the senior manager from his line director, the HR director and others, his authoritarian style does not change.
- *Response*: Towards the end of his six-month probationary period, he is informed that he will not be offered a permanent position and so leaves the Group. Whilst technically very competent, his leadership management style and values do not

align with those of the Group. An internal appointment is subsequently made by promoting the training centre administra-
tor to the position of training manager, which proves to be
very successful in behavioural and financial terms.

Impact on its people: High.

- The interaction between middle management and the company's
  people.

The challenge facing the CEO to overcome the existing highly negative
culture is compounded by the Group occupying a large multi-location
site and having a wide and growing range of multi-country operations;
they grow to a total of 24 offices in 19 countries across the Americas,
Europe, the Middle East and the Asia Pacific. And, at the same, he is
leading the turnaround of an underperforming business in a growing
market for it to become a world leader. The nature of these challenges
varies by stakeholder; from the chairman and vice chairman, the executive team, management and to staff; to the CEO.

The CEO recognises the need to be seen to be demonstrating his tone
on a '360 degrees' basis across the Group. A high level of formal interaction by the CEO across the Group, from the private equity owners (i.e.
with its executives being the chairman and vice chairman of the Group)
to the executive team, managers and staff is introduced (see Box 5.5a).
Likewise, it is reciprocated that the management at all levels has the
opportunity to meet and have conversations with the chairman and vice
chairman. The Group's chairman and vice chairman consequently develop a close understanding of the formal policies and disciplines and informal processes by which the CEO leads the business, that is, whether
the CEO is seen to be successfully demonstrating the right moral tone
from the top.

While this provides a platform for the CEO to demonstrate what is
preferred and unacceptable behaviour, he sees this as being insufficient.

Consequently, arrangements are also put in place by the CEO for the
chairman and vice chairman to have considerable access and exposure
to a wide range of managers and the company's people under different
circumstances, with and without the CEO being present (see Box 5.5b).
The chairman and vice chairman are thus able to gain feedback on the
CEO's modus operandi and the extent to which management below director and staff are completely behind the Group's agreed purpose and
the extent to which it is actually alive in the Group. This is in diametrical

Box 5.5a The CEO's Formal Interaction across the Group

- Chairman and board:
  - Pre-board meeting briefings
  - Monthly board meetings.
- Executive team:
  - Monthly board meetings
  - Monthly financial review and year end forecast meeting
  - Monthly operations meeting
  - Monthly 1-2-1 meetings
  - Quarterly off-site two-day workshops.
- Managers:
  - Annual visit to each country office
  - Annual three-day international conference
  - Biannual briefing session
  - Attendance at workshops
  - Customer site visits.
- Staff:
  - Annual visit to each country office
  - Biannual briefing sessions on the business
  - Attendance at lunch and learn sessions
  - Customer site visits.

Box 5.5b The Chairman's and Vice Chairman's Informal Interactions across the Group

- Meeting directors and senior managers over an informal sandwich lunch after each board meeting.
- Holding one-to-one meetings with directors and managers without the CEO being present.
- Accompanying the CEO on country office visits.
- Participating in the executive team's off-site two-day quarterly workshops, which include dinner and an overnight stay.
- Attending the annual international conference, which brings together senior people from each of the country offices and from HQ (totalling some 50–60 staff). Attendance at the evening dinners, with each of them sitting at separate tables without any other board member being present, and mixing freely in pre- and post-dinner conversations with staff.

Box 5.5c The CEO's Processes for Gauging the Interaction between Middle Management and the Group's People

- The CEO regularly joins workshop sessions as an observer and attends the workshop's informal dinner (see Box 5.5a).
- The annual staff satisfaction survey results are analysed at a highly disaggregated level and are communicated by face-to-face debriefing at the departmental level (see Box 5.5a).
- The UK main site is large and sprawling with two office blocks, the main factory and a very large R&D complex. He introduces a practice of going to managers' offices, following a brief phone call to see if they are available. As executive team and managers' offices are in different buildings across the very large site, the deliberate spin-off from this practice is that the CEO is frequently seen by staff.
- For country offices, CEO's visits include visiting customer sites with local staff, joining the monthly management meetings, presentation update sessions for all staff and the subsequent informal lunch and dinner sessions.
- The informal interactions during the annual international conference also provide a basis for sensing the quality of personal interaction between country offices, their leaders and staff.

---

contrast to how things are done under the prior leadership regime; board meetings are rehearsed in advance of them taking place and the chairman and vice chairman are not given the opportunity to meet managers and staff.

With respect to the critical interaction between middle management and the company's people and execution of the Group's purpose and its strategy, the tone from the middle is more important for staff than the tone from the top. But, the tone from the top sets the tone for the middle. Hence, a CEO must monitor to check what the tone is from the middle. It is also why there is the need for radical engagement and communication with staff.

Box 5.5c sets out the range of processes whereby the CEO is able to gauge the nature and quality of interaction between middle management and the Group's people, and its tone. The processes are based on the CEO's view that staff at all levels should not be surprised to see the CEO in and about the business, is interested in what they actually do, and may actually wish to discuss it personally with them. Over time, the frequency and informal quality of casual conversations with them increases and improves. They get to know him better and he gains a better understanding of the business at the sharp end and the reality of the extent to which the Group's purpose is being lived and implemented by middle management and their people.

The group of executives and managers became a very strong team. They focus on what is good for the Group overall. They set themselves stretching performance targets which they invariably deliver. They are marching to the same drum in successfully executing the Group's purpose and strategy.

A company's people readily recognise a values-based approach to how issues are handled. It sets the culture or bar of 'how things are done around here' and hence how its people should actually engage with their company in all of its activities. It engenders trust between people in the company and with the company. Employees gain increasing confidence in the promulgated culture and values which lead to heightened integrity cascading throughout an organisation as the norm.

Staff: Deliver Radical Staff Engagement and Communication

Staff engagement and communication must be delivered in a fundamentally radical manner. There is the vital need to ensure that employees decode the communication and the way it is intended with respect to the company's purpose, and that management receive contributions in return. It culminates in enlightened empowerment of staff by top management. Leaders give up power and staff make decisions and take actions with confidence. Radical engagement and communication are delivered through interactive face-to-face communication being the norm. It must not be a case of cascading communication. Two-way interaction between leaders and employees requires feedback from colleagues.

The Group's prior culture is completely different: there is little transparency or trust; there is micro-management; it is very hierarchical and secretive; it has a blame culture; it is risk-averse; and communication is often by way of rumours.

In response, a radical change is implemented in all aspects of staff engagement and communication. Box 5.6a sets out some of the processes deployed for fullest engagement of staff primarily through face-to-face communication. So as to place Box 5.5a in its context, Figure 5.1 summarises the Group's comprehensive annual communication programme. Much of it is delivered by face-to-face sessions with an open Q&A forum being a standing practice.

Whilst the Group's former culture is characterised as being highly dysfunctional, a significant number of key management processes and

Box 5.6a Radical Staff Engagement through Face-to-Face Communication

- In terms of engaging staff, a core element of the Group's new comprehensive communication programme (see Figure 5.1) is the holding of open question and answer (Q&A) sessions at all staff events (e.g. workshops, staff satisfaction survey results, staff business briefings, training sessions, lunch and learn sessions).
- The Group's programme of workshops encompasses all of its main activities. Employee participation in workshops is determined on the basis of who is best placed to contribute to and benefit from the subject under investigation, irrespective of staff grade, seniority or country office. This facilitates breaking down the conventional hierarchy of the Group. Workshop subject areas are increasingly decided by employees rather than being handed down by management. At the end of each workshop session, employees (not management) decide which top three to five actions will be taken forward for completion in the subsequent three to six month period, which actions are to be parked for later consideration, and which actions will not be carried out. This is documented, the selected actions are implemented, and then the results and/or failures are reported back in subsequent communication or workshop sessions. Workshops conclude with a Q&A open forum for staff to raise questions and issues, and a workshop satisfaction survey is conducted. Its results are disseminated to all participants directly within 24 hours and reviewed at any subsequent related workshop. Thus, employees are directly involved in identifying the actions to be taken and are given the responsibility and authority to implement the recommendations.
- The face-to-face debriefing of the results of the annual staff satisfaction survey is in terms of the Group as a whole; each country operation and each major function in the business such as capital sales, contract delivery, spares, service, R&D and HQ services (i.e. Finance and HR). Feedback is in terms of what actions have been taken in response to the survey results; what actions are planned to be taken; what is being parked and why; and what extra has been done and what extra is going to be done and why. It is followed in all sessions by an open Q&A forum with employees.

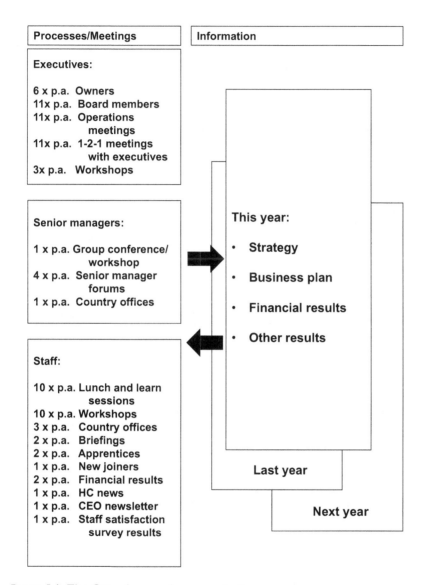

Figure 5.1 The Group's annual communications programme.

controls in place are found by the new CEO to be excellent. In conversations with the company's people at all levels, the CEO refers to them publicly as 'golden nuggets' (see Box 5.6b). The CEO speaks in terms of polishing and enhancing these invaluable cornerstones for delivering the Group's future success. This provides a common positive basis for constructive conversations and thereby facilitates greater initial engagement between the Group's people and its new CEO than may have been anticipated for a newly parachuted-in CEO by a private equity owner. However, the missing element is the core business process for how best to deliver these management control processes; that is, leading and operating the Group with heightened integrity.

In many respects, there is a need to over-communicate and to listen. This seems to be the case for the Group. This is illustrated by, for example, the nicknames given to the CEO by the Group's people. Nicknames provide a tangible demonstration of what staff really think about their CEO and his credibility. They provide illuminating insight into people's perception of the CEO's demonstrated style and behaviour.

The Group's CEO becomes aware of two nicknames: '*We said we would do it, and we're doing it now*' and '*the old man*' (See Box 5.6c). It seems that the CEO resonates with the Group's people in terms of communication and respect.

With this shift to radical engagement and communication with a company's people, then '*How we work around here*' brings a highly positive instead of a highly negative culture. As could be expected, this directly results in reduced staff absenteeism and staff turnover. Box 5.6d shows that the level of staff turnover reduces considerably when it is benchmarked against the Group's UK industry average. It also directly yields significant financial benefits for the Group.

The radical engagement and comprehensive communication programme bring people together which fosters innovation, creativity and a sense of shared responsibility. It reduces the dependency of decisions being preserved to higher levels in the Group's hierarchy. It leads to increases in staff competence to do their job and personal ownership of

---

Box 5.6b 'Golden Nuggets' in the Group's Management Control Processes

- Sales quotation pipeline process.
- Contract bid review process.
- Contract monitoring and review process.
- Handover from sales to contracts teams process.
- Zero-based budget and cost centre process.
- Monthly forecast of latest best estimate year-end results process.
- Over ten years of no regulatory, environmental, and health and safety incidents or fines.

Box 5.6c Nicknames Tell a Lot

- One nickname for the CEO is revealed in circuitous manner. To celebrate the opening of a major investment in R&D facilities, a former UK government minister is invited to 'cut the ribbon'. It is arranged for all staff at the main HQ site to have tea and biscuits in the factory so that the former minister can meet some of them before later addressing all staff on the main site.
- Knowing the former minister's preferred style, he is unaccompanied when meeting staff. He thereby meets whoever he wishes to meet in order to chat informally with them.
- He spends some considerable time with a small group of female staff.
- After the minister moves on to chat with another group of staff, the CEO then goes over and asks them what they thought of the former minister. In addition to saying that he is a charming and well-informed person, they respond by saying he asked them what our nickname is for you.
- The CEO draws his breath and asks what it is.
- They reply that they call him 'We said we would do it, and we're doing it now'.
- They go on to explain that in the regular communication sessions, he always explains what the future plans are and then at subsequent sessions he reports on whether they have been carried out, and that he invariably concludes with the words 'We said we would do it, and we are doing it now'.
- On another occasion when the CEO is on his way to the R&D centre for an informal catch-up briefing with its manager, the manager comments that he was just speaking to some of his people saying that 'the old man' is here soon.
- He pauses somewhat embarrassingly and then goes on to explain that 'the old man' is a term of high respect drawn from his Royal Navy days, where it is used when the captain of the ship has earned the respect of his ship's crew.

---

any recommended changes. It favours inclusion over exclusion. This gives the people in the Group a voice in their work. It demonstrates respect and leads to a very high level of job satisfaction for employees. Employees believe that they are listened to by management and that it takes appropriate action in a positive collaborative manner. They believe that they are trusted and have a sense of belonging.

Box 5.6d Shift to a Positive Culture Results in Substantial Reductions in Staff Turnover and Increases in Financial Returns

- A proxy indicator of a shift from a predominantly negative to a positive culture, and radical engagement with employees, is reductions in staff turnover and absenteeism. The Group's UK firm staff turnover changes dramatically. This is from being slightly higher than the average level of UK engineering sector, to being reduced to less than a third during a period of an increasingly tight labour market.
- Over the same period, the Group's absenteeism remains around a third below that of the average level of UK engineering sector.

	Year 2 (%)	Year 4 (%)
Turnover:		
– Company	14.1	5.8
– UK average	13.5	18.3
Absenteeism:		
– Company	1.4	1.2
– UK average	3.6	3.5

- The financial value generated from these improvements in staff turnover and absenteeism is significant: An annual saving and improvement in cash flow equivalent to 20 per cent of year one profits and the cost savings as increased profits generate a seven per cent point increase in the price achieved for the sale of the Group.
- There are also considerable improvements in staff productivity levels: return on sales increases nearly threefold; revenue per employee increases by 42 per cent; and profit per employee increases by 67 per cent over the seven-year period. These improvements are also underpinned by considerable tangible and intangible investment in the Group.

The Group's leaders and its people become fully aligned for how to go about actual realisation of its defined purpose. If they are not fully aligned, then the Group's purpose could not be delivered nor be sustained. However, radical staff engagement and communication are necessary but not sufficient for the 'Heightened Integrity Model' to actually deliver a company's previously defined purpose.

Feedback: Proactively Close the Feedback Loop between Leaders and the Company's People

Proactively closing the feedback loop between leaders and staff is the imperative for successful delivery of the core business process: The 'Heightened Integrity Model'. The feedback loop has to be independent of management and transparent to all employees. This is because leaders can frame questions so as to influence the response provided by the company's people. Transparent feedback can only be achieved through having open-ended Q&A sessions between leaders and staff, often through holding regular company communication sessions.

Closing the feedback loop constructively between leaders and a company's people creates a culture of speaking up. Leaders as well as employees must deliver and accept constructive feedback, with both criticism and praise being delivered sincerely. This also demonstrates that there is mutual trust and transparency between leaders and the company's people. Importantly, it also provides a clear indicator that operating with heightened integrity is pervading the culture of the company.

The open consumer feedback revolution provides a model for a communication feedback loop which positively engages a company's people. There is a growing number of open consumer review websites such as Booking.com, TripAdvisor, Toptable and Reevoo. The key attributes for successfully adopting open consumer feedback for proactively closing the feedback loop between leaders and a company's people are as follows:

- *Autonomy*: The system must operate independently of management (the system provider) whereby management cannot influence the feedback from staff (the customer).
- *Transparency*: There has to be an open reporting system whereby there is public awareness (i.e. other staff) of what staff are feeding back and, equally, of management's response.
- *Informed feedback*: Staff have to be positioned to raise legitimate issues on an informed basis. It, in turn, requires management to provide staff a full understanding of the business, its performance and prospects.
- *Generate user loyalty*: The system has to be open to allow user generated comments being available to other staff. Here, one member of staff can ask about a subject or issue and other staff members can volunteer to add their views (and also provide helpful responses).

Such a feature helps the creation of loyalty of users as they experience its interactive openness.

- *Right of reply*: In TripAdvisor, hotels and restaurants (the service providers) have a right of reply and can respond to customer feedback. For the pro-integrity business model, it is a requirement that management must reply and must do so transparently to staff.
- *Positive feedback loops*: The emphasis must be on creating positive, constructive two-way engagement of staff and management, resulting in a virtuous circle of successful communication.

This section draws on the framework developed by the international non-governmental organisation 'Integrity Action'. It helps citizens to monitor the delivery of vital projects and services where they live and to solve the problems they find. This is facilitated by use of its technology tool and mobile app called 'DevelopmentCheck'.[1] It is inspired by the rise of open feedback in the commercial sector, which sees consumers posting their feedback publicly, in real time. This shift means their feedback cannot be ignored.

There are, however, substantial differences between the open feedback model for service providers such as restaurants and hotels and the feedback process between employees and management of a company:

- For the open consumer feedback process, consumers have the option of 'exit' in choosing to no longer use the provider (i.e. not to eat at the restaurant again and to use another restaurant, with a negligible opportunity cost to the customer) and the provider has no recourse to act against the user.
- For employees, the decision to 'exit' is exceedingly high (i.e. to resign and find another employer) and they have to have confidence that they can raise issues without fear of a career limiting reaction from management.
- For leaders, it has to ensure that there is a climate of trust where challenging questions on sensitive issues do not lead to rancour or career-limiting ramifications for the staff raising the questions. If this does happen, then the process would no longer be used by staff and it would thereby fail.

Table 5.3 sets out the rating of each of the attributes of open consumer feedback against selected processes for closing the feedback loop between leaders and a company's people. It can be seen that open forum Q&A sessions consistently score higher than, for example, staff satisfaction surveys or workshop sessions.

The inherent weakness of staff satisfaction surveys for proactively closing the feedback loop with integrity is that management controls the type of questions being asked and can frame the presentation of the

Table 5.3 Rating of processes for closing the feedback loop

Attributes	Processes		
	Staff satisfaction surveys	*Workshop sessions*	*Open forum Q & A*
Autonomy	Low	Low	High
Transparency	Low	Low	High
Informal feedback	Medium	High	High
User loyalty	High	High	High
Right of reply	High	High	High
Positive feedback loop	Low	Medium	High

questions and results. To an extent, this could be overcome by outsourcing the survey to a third party. However, management could still filter the response to open-ended questions by subtly framing the narrative being presented back to staff with a resulting different interpretation being made by staff. Lewis (2017) cites, for example, one of the experiments of Kahneman and Amostversby (who are often referred to as the founding fathers of behavioural economics):

- One group of high school students is asked to estimate the product of $8 \times 7 \times 6 \times 5 \times 4 \times 3 \times 2 \times 1$.
- Another group of high school students is asked to estimate the product of $1 \times 2 \times 3 \times 4 \times 5 \times 6 \times 7 \times 8$.
- Both groups are given five seconds to do the exercise.
- The median answer of the first group is 2,250 and that of the second is 512 (with the correct answer being 40,320).

Lewis goes on to explain that the reason the students in the first group guess a higher number is that they use 8 as a starting point, while the students in the second group use 1.

How the exercise is framed, the power of the sequencing of the same numbers, influences the answer.

Consequently, staff satisfaction surveys fail to meet the attributes of 'autonomy' and 'transparency' for a proactive integrity-based feedback loop between staff and management. Management can frame the presentation of questions and responses in such a way that they directly shape how they are interpreted by staff.

The acid test for success of open forum Q&A sessions is the extent to which staff are prepared to ask, and importantly continue to ask, the CEO and other leaders in their company challenging questions and receive publicly meaningful, honest answers. If leaders do not respond in such a manner publicly to challenging questions, then staff will over time stop asking them. Employees will then have little trust or confidence in their CEO or management.

Box 5.7 illustrates the substantive shift from the prior culture of employees effectively being in fear of asking the Group's leaders questions

---

Box 5.7 Closing the Feedback Loop: Challenging Questions to the CEO in an Open Q&A Forum

- At the new CEO's first briefing for the executive team and senior managers from the Group's country offices (in month three of his first year, where the purpose, vision and stretching ambition for the Group are launched), questions are invited by the CEO. None are asked.
- In a subsequent private conversation with a senior member of staff, he is informed that managers are most reluctant to ask the CEO questions as at the previous such session, some three years earlier, the employee who asked the then CEO a challenging question suddenly left the company with no explanation.
- This changes markedly over time as staff gain confidence and trust in the Group's leadership.
- From around the third quarter of year two onwards, the following are typical of the challenging questions that staff publicly ask top management in face-to-face interactions during what becomes the standard open forums for Q&A between staff, management and the CEO:
  - 'Given the dangers of working in Nigeria, are you going to force us to go?'(Service engineers' workshop).
  - 'Who are you selling us to and for how much?' (Staff communication session).
  - 'You've taken away our subsidised hot lunches, our on-site medical centre and now you're taking away our final salary pension. What's next?' (Staff briefing session on planned changes to pension provision).
  - 'Without the launch of the new product you promised a year ago, we're down on our bonus. When are we going to get the new product?' (Sales conference).
  - 'You say that we are growing and profitable, so why are you making redundancies?' (Staff communication session).
- What became the standard response by the CEO to questions in such sessions is that if he knew the answer to a question, then he would give it; if he did not know the answer to a question, then he would say so and find out the answer and report back; and if he did not want to answer a question, then he would say so.

to one where its people regularly ask challenging questions in an open, transparent public forum.

Moreover, the extent to which a company's people ask and continue to ask their leaders challenging questions can become the litmus test for a company's board and its chairperson as to whether their CEO is seen to be leading and operating their company with heightened integrity. By definition, CEOs have high degrees of freedom in how they execute a company's defined purpose and its strategy. Such a litmus test provides a board and its chairperson with a clear yardstick for monitoring how a CEO actually goes about executing delivery of the company's defined purpose. A chairperson's stewardship role is important here for ensuring that the CEO is holding true to delivering the board's previously agreed company purpose, particularly as the tenure of many chairpeople is longer than that of their CEOs.

Consequently, the proactive interaction of leadership's demonstrated tone, radical staff engagement and communication, and closing the feedback loop results in the Group being led and operated with heightened integrity. The Group's leaders and its people are positively aligned and overwhelmingly interact with the highest levels of values, through operating and being seen to operate with transparency and trust.

With successful implementation, the core business process model forms the life blood of the Group. Leading and operating with heightened integrity is the heart pumping the blood to deliver its sustainable purpose.

Note

1 'Integrity Action' provides citizens a practical way to make projects and services local to them work better through monitoring. It gives them power through transparency of feedback. http://integrityaction.org/ https://integrityaction.org/devcheck/. The author is a trustee of 'Integrity Action'.

Reference

Lewis, M. (2017) "*The undoing project: A friendship that changed the world*", Penguin Random House.

Chapter 6

VERIFICATION

Successful Benchmarking of the Model against Third-Party Best Practice

Greater veracity for the 'Heightened Integrity Model' for leading and operating a purpose-defined company and its case study application is gained by successfully benchmarking what it did in practice against third-party best practices, which are as follows:

- The set of five behavioural principles a purpose company must comply with as laid out by the UK-based think-tank, A Blueprint for Better Business (2017).
- The definition and attributes of 'a great place to work' as defined by the US-based company Great Place to Work Institute (Edmans 2012).
- The set of nine measurable business payoffs that a purpose company must meet as laid out by the UK-based think-tank, The Big Innovation Centre (2016).

Throughout the benchmarking, cross-reference is also made to the relevant subprocesses of the core business process model. This provides additional evidence-based argument in substantiation of the model's wider applicability and hence rigor. It also demonstrates that the model's applicability goes beyond a single case study.

Purpose: Behavioural Principles

Blueprint for Better Business (2016) defines a purpose company in behavioural terms by its five principles which characterise the '*what*' that is required of a purpose company. They are as follows: having a purpose which delivers long-term sustainable performance for the economy and society; being a responsible and responsive employer; being honest and fair with customers and suppliers; being a guardian for future generations; and being a good citizen. Blueprint for Better Business presents the rationale for the five principles with comprehensive evidence-based arguments in terms of the benefits of following them for a company's performance.

The first guiding principle can only be delivered if the subsequent four guiding principles are in place. These are therefore considered first. Whether the case study corporation delivers its defined purpose in terms of the first guiding principle (of long-term sustainable performance for the economy and society) is the subject of Chapter 7.

... being a responsible and responsive employer...

For a company to be a responsible and responsive employer, it is necessary to treat staff with dignity, to encourage leadership and personal accountability through greater transparency and trust. There is a need to go beyond the minimum and build trusting relationships. Central to this is empowerment of staff. Here, leaders give up power and staff take decisions and are responsible for the ensuing actions. Such trusting relationships have to be between the company and its people and the people themselves.

Box 6.1a summarises the Group's prior adverse culture of how it treats its people as a resource with little respect of them as individuals. Box 6.1b sets out a unique step to empower individual employees. This is in terms of rectifying the imbalance of knowledge and information and, hence, power in an organisation through ensuring all the Group's people have unfettered access to all core data and documentation. It is accessed via an industry-first internet-based virtual private network called the 'Knowledge Bank'.

Figure 6.1 presents an overview of the Knowledge Bank in terms of the activities it encompasses (i.e. sales, operations, services, spares and corporate information) and the extensive and highly commercially sensitive information available against each of these categories of activities. This ranges from all customer quotes and related cost and technical details, to over 40,000 files of engineering drawings, data on 20,000 installations at over 9,000 customer sites, and operations and maintenance manuals for all in-house and outsourced components and products. In business discussions with a Fortune 500 multinational, it describes the 'Knowledge Bank' as a 'world beater', in that the corporation said it had tried to do the same but had failed.

Box 6.1c provides an example of the use of the 'Knowledge Bank' by staff at a customer's site some 100 km from the São Paulo office in Brazil. Its use at the client's installation enables what is ostensibly a complaint being transformed into an example of superb customer service through empowering staff with immediate access to the required customer specific installation information. The Knowledge Bank proves to be a powerful tool for empowering the Group's people and delivering superior customer service in real time.

Box 6.1a The Group's Prior People Culture

- The Group essentially uses people as resources to achieve its financial objectives. Its culture is highly dysfunctional. It is largely command and control, and hierarchical. There is little trust and employee morale is very poor.
- Long-term serving staff are leaving the Group due to frustration in their jobs. New joiners often leave quickly due to the Group's archaic, hierarchical command-and-control and blame culture. Staff turnover is above the industry average. Staff contracts and terms and conditions are inconsistent and in a mess. It is not a learning organisation and innovation is not encouraged. Country offices and their people are treated by HQ and many senior staff as second-class citizens in subservient satellite offices.

Box 6.1b Empowering Individual Employees by the Group's 'Knowledge Bank'

- Knowledge and information is power in an organisation. There is an imbalance of power between staff where one party controls and holds information and data.
- For the Group, there is an asymmetrical imbalance of access to information and data between staff and business needs due to its hierarchical structure and the second-class citizenship of its country offices. This imbalance is accentuated as the Group expands substantially in geographic coverage and in staff numbers outside the UK. Many staff have less than three years' experience with the company and most of these staff are in country offices some distance from the Group's main UK operations (which had increased from 13 to 20 country companies in 19 countries with 24 offices in total).
- Consequently, this leads to an accentuated technical and, hence, financial risk due to an imbalance of information.
- To correct this imbalance, all employees irrespective of their location are provided with unfettered access to all core data and documentation. An internet-based virtual private network is established, with online access by all country offices and staff irrespective of their location. It is badged the 'Knowledge Bank'.

- Figure 6.1 provides a summary of its contents. It is structured as a library. Its contents are organised in terms of the Group's five main product or market sectors (with a common index across them) along with a section on corporate matters. All employees are able both to withdraw data and documentation from it and to deposit additional data and documentation with the completion of new contract sales and installations, spares and service, and results of R&D tests projects. Access to it is just by two keyboard clicks.

- For commercial security purposes, access is tracked overtly by each user having a personal log-on code and covertly centrally in terms of monitoring 'excessive' accessing or downloading of commercially sensitive information.

Activity	Information	
Sales	Sales literature	Brochures and over 70 product data sheets
	Customer profile	Reference listing and customer "quotes"
	Visualisation	Flares, static pictures, video footage, animated views, exploding views
	Documentation	Bid review, LOI authorisations, credit requests
	Costs	Cost book, lead times
Operations	Manuals	O&M manuals, supplier manuals, test certificates, accreditations
	Drawings	3DCAD images, standard GA's, burner application, fuel supply, oil, gas, ancillaries, electrical standards, schematics, 3 Ph3
	Data	Sizing programmes, data sheet, burner application, ancillaries, control, 40,000+ files of engineering drawings
	Documentation	Sales/contract handover, contract/supply chain handover, contract/service handover supplier assessment inspection, expediting reports, material certifications, packing specifications, test procedures
Services	Data	Service reports, commission reports, standard service pro forma, site work assessment, risk assessment, method statement, bid reviews, internal transfers, commissioning transfers
Spares	Data	Exploded views, drawing reference lists, standard price lists, installed database of 20,000 + contracts for 9,000 + customer sites
	Documentation	Certificate of conformance, certificate of origin, bid review
General	Documentation	Quality manuals, PINs, suggestion schemes

Figure 6.1 Overview of the Knowledge Bank

Box 6.1c Transforming a Complaint to Superior Customer Service through Employee Empowerment via the 'Knowledge Bank', Brazil

- The 'Knowledge Bank' provides all employees with remote access to more than 80 per cent of core data and documentation held by the Group. Connectivity between staff increases as they all have the same access to core data, information and documentation. It dramatically reduces the imbalance of information and hence power between staff, particularly between HQ-based employees and employees in country offices. It results in empowerment of country offices and staff.

• By way of example of its use, during the visit by the CEO and local colleagues to a customer's chemical process plant some 100 km from the São Paulo office in Brazil, the client's resident engineer points out that a piece of equipment recently supplied has three holes in it, which apparently has to accommodate five wires. On inspection of the installation and taking its drawing number, the original 3D CAD drawing is brought up on the local colleague's personal computer via the Knowledge Bank. The 3D CAD drawing is rotated and the individual part identified. It quickly becomes apparent that the client has unfortunately cited the wrong part number in his order, as is evident from the drawing and the client's order form, which is also brought up on the system. The part is identified and immediately ordered by email with confirmation by return that it will be delivered in less than five working days. The client is visibly impressed.

Being a responsible employer requires balancing empowering staff whilst at the same time mitigating the attendant risk to the company. Empowering a company's people with unfettered access to all core data and documentation comes with it a fundamental risk. This is especially so for highly decentralised multinational corporations and especially where country managers are encouraged to be entrepreneurial. Country leaders may unwittingly draw on such readily available technical and commercial information and use it to enter commercial contracts where they have little direct experience – particularly for a company where absolute safety of its highly technical products is paramount (i.e. combustion burners are essentially a controlled explosion of fuels).

To mitigate this risk whilst still empowering local leaders and their people, there is a need for a structured and transparent process for country company offices and staff to move up the value chain of their multinational company's activities in a disciplined manner and in accordance with its overall strategy.

The objective here is for local leaders of country companies to be entrepreneurial and to develop their local business plans for their respective countries in a manner that is consistent and coherent with their Group's purpose, strategy and business plans. This leads to considerable decentralisation of company's activities and greater proximity to customers. It generates greater buy-in from staff in the 'home' country of the multinational, in that they can in many respects define and deliver their own destiny within their parent company's overall strategy and defined purpose.

For the case study Group, a 'Country Development Route Map' is designed and implemented. Its objective is to engender disciplined decentralisation and local ownership of decision-making and business activities within a predefined coherent and transparent framework and in alignment with the Group's defined purpose, strategy and business plans. Management and staff in country offices then enjoy richer jobs, real empowerment and greater career prospects than if they operate merely as satellite offices to a distant national headquarters.

Box 6.1d sets out the main features of the 'Country Development Route Map' in terms of activities encompassed, classification of levels of expertise, documentation requirements and responsibility for authorisation levels. It provides a vehicle for country leaders to define and deliver their own destiny.

Positive adoption of the framework by country mangers leads to considerable local specialisation by the Group's country offices in response to their own local expertise and market demand, and in alignment with the Group's purpose and strategy, whilst ensuring that there is no inefficient duplication of expertise across the Group. Box 6.1e summarises the subsequent resulting specialisation of the Group's main country offices. They become an integrated network of country offices with decentralised, not hierarchical, execution aligned by and to the Group's purpose.

Box 6.1d The Group's 'Country Development Route Map' for Country Leaders to Define and Deliver Their Own Destiny

- Activities are classified as 'sales', 'spares', 'service', 'product engineering' and 'product subcontract'.
- Levels of technical and commercial requirements are defined and expressed as 'platinum', 'gold', 'silver' and 'bronze' in descending order of their complexity.
- Documentation covers
  - The controls for the process and the mechanism used to audit that the integrity and consistency of approach is being maintained.
  - The precise boundary conditions for moving a country office from one category to another.
- Responsibility to grant and monitor the category for the country is vested in the executive directors responsible for sale of new products, engineering and spares and service, respectively.

Overall, through the processes and practices set out in Boxes 6.1a–e, the Group's people are empowered to define and deliver their own destiny in accordance with its purpose, vision and strategy. They form and illustrate the 'Heightened Integrity Model's '*radical engagement and communication with staff*'.

An integral element of being a responsive and responsible employer is that sometimes the CEO takes difficult decisions that may not enjoy overall employee support. Even when a company is growing, redundancies and closures can often occur due to changes in a company's market and the need to adjust the company to a new operating state for continuing success. Such actions can be for the overall benefit of the company and its people for contributing to business viability and success over the longer term. But, they invariably have a negative impact on a company's people and their view of its leadership. Box 6.1f summarises some of the hard decisions that were taken in terms of a series of redundancies, office closures and trade union issues.

The critical point here is how these decisions are implemented.

Box 6.1e Resulting Specialisation of Country Offices

- *Group Centres of Excellence*: UK, power, process, marine sectors and hot water and steam raising; Hamworthy Peabody US power sector; and Italy, large-scale flares contracts.
- *South* Korea: The marine sector and the outsourcing locally of the major fabrication works for the Amoxsafe burner for liquefied natural gas carriers and for the flares sector generally.
- Brazil: The power and process sectors, serving the country's large agro-industrial base and Petrobras' interests.
- Poland: The power sector across Eastern Europe.
- Singapore: Service hub for the marine sector.
- Dubai: Marketing for process and flares sectors along with a marine service capability for the Middle East.
- China: Sub-contracting outsourcing centre along with serving the growing number of Chinese corporations that were internationalising their activities.
- France: Gas-rich, French-speaking North African countries.
- Spain: Smaller-scale flares and process contracts.
- Houston, US: US multinationals in the flares and process sectors.

Box 6.1f Decisions and Actions Having an Adverse Impact on the Group's People

- Year 1:
  - Australian company: Closure.
  - US company: Redundancies.
- Year 2:
  - UK company: Trade unions issue a 'Failure to Agree Notice' with respect to moving factory personnel onto a monthly instead of a weekly salary payment system. It is subsequently implemented with the support of the trade unions.
  - South Africa company: Closure.
- Year 3:
  - UK company: Redundancies.
  - UK company: Trade unions issue a 'Failure to Agree Notice' with respect to annual salary increments being changed from a flat level for all staff to having a personal performance element in annual salary increments. It is subsequently implemented with the support of the trade unions.
- Year 5:
  - Dutch company: Sold.
  - UK company: Change in the company's staff pension scheme from 'defined benefits' (where the company bares the risk of the actual pension paid to retired staff) to 'money purchase' (where the employee bares the risk of the actual amount received at retirement). It is implemented with the support of the trade unions.
- Year 6:
  - UK company: Redundancies, with support of the trade unions.

- Box 6.1g provides an overview of how, for example, the South African country office is closed in a sympathetic manner that also offers opportunities to the local staff.
- Box 6.1h sets out the actions leading to redundancies in the US office through local empowerment of its leaders in setting out their own business plan for a company that they would be proud of.

As the closure and redundancies are made in the new CEO's first year or so in post, he is closely watched by the Group's people in terms of how these decisions are taken and implemented; importantly, whether they are taken with authentic sadness, compassion and sympathy.

Box 6.1g Handling a Country Office Closure, South Africa

- Towards the end of year one of the CEO being in post, it is evident that the South African operation is making a loss and has no prospects of a turnaround to profitability. It is the first office to be closed under the new management regime, notwithstanding the stated strategy of growth of the Group through international expansion. In addition, as it is the first overseas office that had been opened by the Group, there is considerable emotion at stake for some of the longer-serving employees.
- The CEO arranges for him and the newly appointed Human Resources (HR) executive director to visit the South African office for a week. After briefing the staff on the reasons for the office closure, several other announcements are made including that:
  - The office will be made available at no cost to all staff for private use until the lease expires (which is some six months away).
  - All staff can retain for their own use company property, cars and PCs etc.
  - A core team, if staff so wish to form one, is offered an exclusive agency agreement with the Group to serve the South African market.
  - The oldest member of staff (in his 70s) and a pregnant administrative officer are retained to sell off the stock of spares on their existing salary plus a generous commission on all stock sold.
- The CEO and HR director do not make a short 'flying visit' to make the announcement and then depart. Instead, they make themselves available throughout their week-long stay so as to be available for one-to-one sessions with individual staff in order to respond to their concerns and to assist in any practical manner as far as is possible.

Box 6.1h Empowering a Country Office, US

- In the first weeks of the CEO taking up the position, a major issue is the losses from its US company. These have reduced the Group's prior year profitability by some 25 per cent. The losses are already common knowledge to many of the Group's senior staff. Not surprisingly, this results in the CEO, accompanied by the Group's board chairman, visiting the US operations in his first month. As there is no incumbent manager and prior to the visit, the CEO contacts the former country manager to try to learn more about the US-based business. He is informed by the prior country manager that there is no suitable internal successor.

- On visiting the office and its engineering facilities, the CEO and chairman meet the two most senior local staff and invite them to dinner that evening. Before the dinner, the chairman asks the CEO for his view. The CEO proposes to appoint the two senior staff to run the company and for them to produce a business plan within four weeks for his return. His reasoning is that a viable US operation will add value for the subsequent sale of the Group as an international business. And, if the Group leaves the US, it will be that much more difficult to establish operations in the country at a later date. And the other options of closure or fire sale will still be available if needed later.

- Over dinner, the CEO informs the two employees of their new roles, president and vice president of US operations, and the requirement to produce a business plan. They ask for its objectives. The CEO's response is that it must be stretching in ambition, be achievable and with the sole criterion of resulting in a business that they will be proud of.

- The CEO returns four weeks later and approves the business plan in its totality. The plan includes redundancies in order to reduce the cost base and to enable the recruitment of new staff with the experience and capabilities to address the US market (which they have not been allowed to do before) and thereby serve customer needs and grow the business.

- The CEO invites this new country management team to present their business plan to the Group's first international conference for senior managers, to be held in the following month. In so doing, it marks a major shift in style of communication; it is being open about what is taking place, why and how the plan is formulated, and demonstrating it is clearly owned and presented by the country management responsible for its implementation. The senior team of the country company is empowered in an open and transparent manner.

In both cases, the CEO is seen to be involved personally in face-to-face meetings locally. From a staff perspective across the Group's international network of offices, the CEO appears to have 'walked the talk' by acting with integrity in a proactive manner. The open reporting and a positive narrative from affected employees on how the changes are presented and implemented in a sympathetic manner signal a dramatic turnaround to senior and other staff in terms of transparent communications.

The CEO felt it is important that when necessarily taking hard business decisions, he should be seen to be delivering them personally and in a sensitive and sympathetic manner. In terms of the 'Heightened Integrity Model', the CEO is then *demonstrating the right moral tone from the top.* With the US office reporting and owning the redundancies in having initiated them and reporting back publicly the process and results at the Group's international conference, it also provides an example of the core business process model's *proactively close the feedback loop between leaders and the company's people.*

Overall, the Group's practices as a responsible and responsive employer lead to its people having the freedom and information to take on the risk of decision-making and contribute to making decisions at all levels. Where previously there is asymmetry of information and power imbalance, there is now empowerment of country offices and all their people. They are neither inferior nor subservient to HQ-located employees. With trust and using knowledge and capabilities, employees increasingly become sources of ideas and innovation, which also increases their job opportunities. With increased openness, employees enjoy richer jobs with greater fulfilment, self-worth and career prospects. These collectively accelerate the actual delivery of the Group's purpose.

Moreover, the focus by Blueprint for Better Business on people with its "*Each person is a someone, not a something...*" and "*... being a responsible and responsive employer...*" reinforces one of the basic tenets of the core business process model. The key connection that matters in a company's stakeholders for the delivery of its defined purpose is its people. Individuals must be treated with respect, mutually collaborative relationships must be built and trust must become the norm between individuals and the company for each person to be a someone, and not to be a something.

A 'Responsible and responsive employer' is then well positioned to deliver on '...being honest and fair with customers and suppliers', '... being a guardian for future generation', and '...being a good citizen'. These guiding principles are exceedingly difficult to adhere to unless employees are on the front foot in terms of their trust in their company's leaders and its culture of trust and transparency with reciprocity between leaders and their people.

... being honest and fair with customers and suppliers...

Due to the very nature of its business, it was in the Group's self-interest *to seek to build lasting relationships with customers and suppliers; deal honestly with customers, providing good and safe products and services; treats suppliers fairly, pays promptly what it owes and expect it suppliers to do the same; and openly share its knowledge to enable customers and suppliers to make better informed choices.*

For the Group, it would not be unexpected that in operating predominantly in the challenging downstream oil and gas sector, and offering products and services involving combustion burners (which are essentially controlled explosions), there can be dangerous incidents at client sites.

A specific aspect of the challenge facing the Group in being honest and fair with customers and suppliers is that in responding to any one incident it could involve a number of parties. The cause of an incident could be the Group's combustion burners and/or the customer's operating regime and/or the facilities' installation contractor at the same time. Box 6.2a describes the complexity of customer/supplier relationships particularly with respect to identifying the cause of poor or dangerous combustion burner performance which could result in explosions and destruction of a client's installation with ensuing pollution of the environment.

Box 6.2a Complexity of Customer and Supplier Relationships

- The Group's products are bespoke in terms of burner performance and its integration with the client's specific application. Adverse performance could lead to substantial damage from explosions with resultant pollution of the environment and risk to lives.
- The Group's products generally form but a small component of the end-user's facility. Installation is often by a third party (the engineering, procurement and construction contractor [EPC]). Consequently, when incidents do occur, it is rare that the cause and hence responsibility for the incident is immediately self-evident. It can be due to operational matters (end-user responsibility), the installation (EPC responsibility), or the combustion burner itself (the Group's responsibility), or due to any combination of the three. And, a further complexity is that the parties rarely have a common financial objective.

Box 6.2b Former Regime's Response to Incidents at Client Installations: Reactive and Adversarial

- When there is an 'incident' at a client's installation under the previous management regime, there is the requirement up front to obtain a written agreement from the end-user for a site visit from the Group's specialists and agreement for the cost of the visit to be underwritten as a cost to the client, unless it is subsequently proven that the Group's equipment is responsible for the incident. It is adversarial and reactive.
- Not unexpectedly, this often leads to a tortuous negotiation, client dissatisfaction and Group staff going to client sites for investigations being on the back foot, usually arriving sometime after the incident and not necessarily being welcomed.

Box 6.2b summarises the former regime's policy for responding to incidents at client installations. It frequently results in an adverse client relationship, irrespective of whether or not the Group is subsequently found to be responsible for the incident.

Box 6.2c sets out the new regime's policy for responding to incidents at client installations. This leads to a fundamental shift in the interrelationship between the company and its suppliers and customers, from an adversarial one to a collaborative one by operating on the front foot in a pro-active, open and honest manner with suppliers and customers.

The positive collaborative nature extends beyond responding to incidents at customer installations. It also includes one-to-one contract negotiations with clients, with an example presented in Box 6.2d. Here a situation of threatened litigation is transformed to a position of first-class client satisfaction, as evidenced by the award of additional contracts.

Box 6.2c New Regime's Response to Incidents at Client Installations: Proactive and Collaborative

- Under the new leadership regime, it is agreed to reverse the position with the challenge of turning what could be a negative interaction with a client into a positive one by taking a proactive response to incidents.
- As soon as any staff member becomes aware of an incident, they report it immediately to their country manager and to the Sales or Contracts executive directors at HQ. If an incident occurs in the

country where the Group has an office, then two local staff are dispatched immediately with clear instructions to photograph as much as possible of the incident site and to interview site local staff as to what has happened. In addition, two senior combustion specialists are sent to the site to follow the Group's agreed policies and processes for conducting an incident investigation.

- The client is informed by email that the Group is taking this action, that any costs involved will be discussed at the conclusion of the investigation and after the client has received and commented on the Group's investigation team's report. In the email to the end-user, there is no request for permission from the client for Group staff to make a visit or to conduct an investigation. It is taken as a given.
- In the overwhelming majority of cases, the end-user welcomes the Group's investigation report. On most occasions, the client meets in full the invoice for the Group's investigation team's time, costs and expenses.

Box 6.2d From Threatened Litigation to First-Class Client Satisfaction

- The Group has successfully sold to a blue-chip UK-based multinational corporation a set of combustion burners that was specified to meet the client's exacting operational performance criteria. However, after an 18-month period of operations, it is increasingly clear that the burner set is not performing to the required specification and that the client might start litigation to recover cash and operational performance losses.
- A meeting is arranged with the client's mainboard director and its purchasing director. The following proposition is tabled to the client: to set up a joint working team made up of the customer's combustion burner specialist with a counterpart from the Group; to define within six months how the client's exacting operational requirements could be met; then to design and engineer the required combustion burner; and then test it extensively at the Group's R&D centre. The cash costs of the work are to be met by the Group, and the customer is to own all intellectual property rights and patents.
- It is agreed to proceed on this basis. However, at the end of the six-month period, there is no success. There is joint realisation that the client's requirements are not technically feasible.

> • Nevertheless, shortly afterwards the client finalises a major purchase order for different combustion sets from the Group. The client states that this is on the basis that best endeavours have been taken by the Group in a transparent manner and that it does not walk away from customer problems.

The result of these processes and practices is that overall customer satisfaction shifts dramatically from being very poor to one of being excellent. Such a fundamental shift in customer satisfaction is clearly evident in the results of independent surveys of a cross-section selection of some 80 customers carried out in year two and then in year five by the same specialist market research company (see Box 6.2e).

In being honest and fair with customers and suppliers, the Group is truly serving them and creating a sense of shared responsibility. The Group's service to customers and suppliers is excellent. The basis of this shift is simple: acting with integrity in all matters with suppliers and customers. As such, it serves to illustrate the subprocess of *'embed an integrity /compliance ethos throughout the company'* of the core business process model. Additionally, with the Group's investigation teams now being welcomed on client sites, this underpins the delivery of *radical engagement and communication of staff* through their high level of proactive collaboration with customers and suppliers, as required by the Group's defined purpose.

Box 6.2e Fundamental Shift to Excellent Client Satisfaction

• Towards the end of year two, a specialist third-party company is retained to conduct market research and to assess customer satisfaction. A cross section of 80 customers across the Group's five main product sectors and a wide range of geographies are interviewed. The findings reveal very high levels of customer dissatisfaction for a variety of reasons.

• In year five, the survey is repeated by the same market research company. The findings are remarkably different. A consistently high level of customer satisfaction is found with not one issue or complaint.

• The market survey company notes that if it had not conducted both surveys, it would not believe that such a dramatic turnaround in customer satisfaction has occurred.

Importantly, it also directly contributes to delivery of the Group's defined purpose. It yields substantial improvement in the operational performance of its combustion burners, which are now world leading. Employees are increasingly welcomed at customer installations in a positive collaborative manner. This results in both greater job satisfaction for employees and improved operational performance of client installations with reduced emissions (cleaner air), greater fuel efficiency (reduced costs and depletion of natural resources) and greater safety (fewer polluting incidents) for the benefit of customers, the environment and society, thereby contributing to the long-term sustainable performance of the economy.

... being a guardian for future generations...

The Group's purpose directly relates to '*its duty of protecting the natural world and conserving finite resources*' through offering its clients market-leading performance combustion burners. That is, the Group's purpose is to:

- Deliver world-leading, cost-effective combustion burners and related services to reduce emissions and increase fuel efficiency with absolute safety.
- Provide technical solutions for reducing the adverse environmental impact of companies operating predominantly in the global, dynamic and generally noxious downstream oil and gas sectors.
- Benefit society with products and services that result in cleaner air and reduced depletion of natural resources in a long-term sustainable manner.
- Contribute to a healthier environment for society and become a guardian of the environment.

Being a guardian for future generations and serving society demands innovation to achieve the Group's purpose as well as financial returns. For delivery of the Group's purpose and to be world leading, the fundamental prerequisite is ensuring a step change increase in the scale of its R&D activities and substantial improvement in the operational performance of its combustion burners.

Pivotal for achieving this objective is a change in the Group's processes for how it goes about its R&D activities along with substantial investment in R&D facilities:

- Box 6.3a summarises the key changes in the Group's processes so that a disciplined strategy of investment in R&D facilities results in world-leading combustion performance.

- Box 6.3b outlines the large scale and range of investment in R&D facilities, which clients subsequently state publicly that they are world-leading facilities.
- Box 6.3c sets out the resulting world-leading products for four of the Group's five main market sectors.
- This considerable investment in R&D processes and facilities also results in substantial financial returns for the Group, as presented in Box 6.3d.

Box 6.3a Radical Changes in R&D Objectives and Processes

- The Group is not initially positioned to deliver its stated purpose. There is little history or experience of R&D efforts resulting in market-leading combustion burner performance. It has not released a major new product for some ten years. Its R&D centre and facilities are not fit for purpose to deliver the Group's ambitions as they are suffering from significant underinvestment.
- Under the prior leadership regime, all R&D is tightly controlled by the then highly risk-averse incumbent CEO.
- An almost diametrically opposed process for setting R&D priorities is introduced by the new CEO. A group-wide committee is established early in year one. Its membership includes the core technical R&D team from the UK, representatives from sales (for a customer perspective) and contracts (for costing and production engineering perspectives), and the senior combustion experts from the US, Italian and French country offices.
- The Group's purpose and vision become the disciplined drivers of R&D investment decisions and are supported by the much-required substantial investment in R&D facilities. The strategy agreed for R&D new product development and roll-out is that each of the Group's main market sectors will have at least one major product that is the leader in performance terms that can be expected to last for at least three to five years. And that all other major products in each market sector have, as a minimum, comparable technical and cost performance to competitor products.

Box 6.3b Substantial Investment in R&D Facilities

* The capital investment in R&D facilities is substantial. It forms the overwhelming majority of total tangible and intangible investment which also includes investment in technology, country offices, apprenticeships and a bespoke technical training centre.
* Total investment is equivalent to an annual run rate of circa 25 per cent of year one profits.
* This includes investment in five additional test rigs (which are very large steel structures); upgrading the ten existing rigs in terms of controls and measurement systems; real-time rather than manual measurement of burner tests; computational fluid dynamics being used for initial burner design; and a customer centre for hosting customers when witnessing the testing of the burners for their contracts.
* By year five, clients recognise and publicly state that the R&D facilities are world leading. The Group is at the cutting edge of R&D with its innovation and technological advances.

Box 6.3c Achieves Product Market Leadership

* Market leadership is achieved for four of the Group's five product markets sectors with clear blue water in terms of performance over its competitors, meeting or exceeding new demanding legislative emission requirements and performing with increased fuel efficiency:
  - Marine sector: Leadership as evident by a dominant market share for its Amoxsafe burner for LNG carriers.
  - Power sector: Its new burner, Ecojet, is recognised and accorded the status of 'latest best technology' in the US.
  - Process sector: A European client states in his presentation at a major international conference that the ESP burner 'is the best burner in the world'.
  - Flares and TOS sector: A threefold increase in the average value of mini-EPC contracts won demonstrates considerable success whilst not necessarily achieving a market-leading position.

Box 6.3d Substantial Financial Returns from R&D Investment

- The investment in the R&D processes and facilities also result in substantial financial success. The returns on the new processes and investment exceed expectations.
- A twofold increase in the average size of contracts is achieved in four of the five main product sectors. The return on investment in R&D from new product development is substantial at slightly circa 500 per cent on the basis of a proxy indicator.*

Growth in average contract size GBP £'000

Market sector	Average contract size	
	Year 3	Year 5
Flares	250–1,500	5,000
Process	350+	750+
Marine	0.5–2,000	5,000
Power	350+	500
Industrial	Catalogue sale	

* The rate of return on investment is measured at the company level as net profit after depreciation as a percentage of average capital employed. The cited return is based on a proxy indicator of gross margin contribution from the sale of new products released over a five-year term as a percentage of total capital invested in R&D facilities over seven years.

The world-leading performance of the company's combustion burners leads to big increases in the volume and size of contracts. It is now able to have much greater impact than previously in improving the quality of the atmosphere around client installations, reducing their use of fossil fuels and the likelihood of polluting disasters, thereby reducing harm to society and promoting its economic sustainability. This also over time leads to competitors stepping up their game in delivering such societal benefits from their installations through having competitively performing combustion burners or they would lose out in winning contracts. Hence, there is clear alignment between the company's purpose, its performance and what it stood for. The Group's purpose shapes and focuses its investment strategy and the commercial and technical performance of its products.

… being a good citizen…

Blueprint for Better Business's 'consider each person affected by its decisions as if he or she were a member of each decision maker's own *community*' can be illustrated by how a corporation acts in exceptional circumstances when its people face unexpected and often emotionally challenging personal situations outside their workplace life. It also serves to demonstrate that each person is being treated as someone; an individual not a resource or factor of production. This can be signalled and is evident by how a company goes the employer's extra mile (as distinct to the too often expectation of employees going the extra mile).

For the Group, this requires a sea change in culture and style as to how it views and treats its people. Box 6.4a provides an illustration of this. Box 6.4b also gives a wide range of individual examples of the Group going the extra mile when some of its people face exceptional personal circumstances, with there not ordinarily being a need for the Group to respond if it was not a purpose-driven company.

Box 6.4a A Sea Change in How the Group's People Are Viewed: The 90th Anniversary Book

- For the Group, a sea change in the style as to how staff are viewed becomes evident early in year one.
- As part of the celebration of the 90th anniversary of the founding of the Group, an upmarket 'coffee table' glossy book is produced. Its unique features include the following:
  - The names of all employees, neither by hierarchy nor by country, but in alphabetical order on the inside front and rear back pages.
  - The smallest office (Canada) having the largest photograph of their people in the book and the executive leadership team having the smallest photograph in the book.
  - All staff and many customers and suppliers receive and welcome copies of the book.

Box 6.4b The Group Goes the Extra Mile for Individuals Who Face Exceptional Personal Problems Outside Their Workplace Life

- An employee is suddenly diagnosed with cancer with only a few weeks left to live. Her mother is disabled and lives several hundred miles away. In order that they are be able to see each other for a last time, arrangements are made at the Group's expense for a private ambulance to take the employee to see her mother.

- A long-serving employee, who has a job in the factory that requires heavy lifting duties, suffers a serious heart attack. It transpires that he has been living for years with a malfunction in his heart and the attack is not due to his workload. His wife visits the office in order to bring in his medical certificate. She is obviously emotionally upset and very worried as to whether her husband will still have a job if he recovers from his heart attack but could not take on his former duties and consequently not meet their mortgage payments and children's university costs. She is assured by the HR Director personally that a job will be found for her husband when he is medically discharged, irrespective of whether he is fit enough to take up his former position and it will be with the same salary.
- At the funeral of a factory worker who had retired several years earlier, a colleague explains to a senior director present (representing the Group) that the widow is becoming increasingly stressed as she is the executor of her deceased husband's will, but she does not know what being an executor entails. She is told to send the will to the Group's lawyer and it will be resolved on the Group's account.
- A member of staff is diagnosed with motor neuron disease. He is increasingly incapacitated and restricted to a wheelchair. With his agreement, a part-time three-day week position is identified for him. With further incapacitation, it is agreed that he will attend the office as and when he feels up to it, without any reduction in his terms and conditions of employment and salary. He subsequently comes to work on an ad hoc basis until he is too frail to do so.

In terms of Blueprint for Better Business's making a '*full and fair contribution to society by structuring its business or operations to pay promptly all taxes that are properly due*', the Group has an apparent clean bill of health in terms of statutory tax returns.

However, in year one a possible exposure in terms of the Group's then transfer pricing policy is evident, as outlined in Box 6.5a. Box 6.5b describes how the exposure is rectified. A further example of reactive compliance is the decision of not to evade a Bank of India ruling on royalty payments by using a circuitous route, as presented earlier in Box 5.4a. The decision not to supply kit to Iran from the Group's US company via its Italian company, even though not currently illegal, is an example of proactive compliance of not avoiding future likely legislation (see Box 5.4c).

The Group is seen by its people as being a good citizen in neither not evading nor avoiding taxes due and governmental legislation.

Being a good citizen contributes to building relationships and communities within the workplace and with society. It brings people together and fosters innovation and a sense of shared responsibility. It underpins and responds to the need of employees wanting fulfilment and greater

---

Box 6.5a Transfer Pricing Exposure

- An exposure in terms of transfer pricing is evident in year one. The Group's country operations are structured as individual profit centres reporting to different executive board directors, whose annual bonus is partially driven by the profit performance of their countries.
- When reviewing the business rationale of the very large number of cost centres in the Group and the transfers between them, it appears that some of the costs are allocated so as to deliver increased profits for specific country offices.

Box 6.5b Transfer Pricing Resolution: Neither Evasion nor Avoidance

- The prior transfer pricing regime could have been deemed to result in inappropriate levels of taxes being paid by certain country operations and with the UK operations. It could be viewed as legal tax avoidance as distinct to illegal tax evasion.
- Nevertheless, a major rationalisation exercise of the allocation of costs between country company office cost centres is undertaken on an arm's length.
- Costs and revenues are then booked to where they rise and fall – with clear transparency and adherence to OECD transfer pricing guidelines – along with associated payment of taxes due. That is, there is now a clear business logic to the Group's transfer pricing that is also compliant with regulatory requirements.
- Shortly after completing this transfer pricing rationalisation and at very short notice, there is an inspection from the UK HM Revenue and Customs authority. In its report of the review, the Group is congratulated on the transparency of its transfer pricing between its country company operations. A number of minor administrative improvements are recommended and are readily implemented.

self-worth from their job in terms of aspiring to meet a wider societal goal. Again, this contributes significantly to furthering the requirements of *'radical engagement and communication with staff'* of the 'Heightened Integrity Model'.

Additionally, making a full and fair contribution to society by structuring its business or operations to pay promptly all taxes that are properly due is clearly seen by staff as part of *'ensuring that leadership's moral compass is seen to demonstrate the right moral tone from the top'*, and, that the Group is *'embodying an integrity and compliance ethos in the business'* for delivery of its defined purpose.

Purpose: Great Place to Work

Further substantiation of the 'Heightened Integrity Model' by its case study demonstration is clearly evident when it is shown to be a great place to work.

The Great Place to Work for Institute (Edmans 2012) defines a *'great place to work'* as one where *'employees trust the people they work for, have pride in what they do, and enjoy the people they work with'*. Such a summary statement is now applicable to the people of the Hamworthy Combustion Group.

In the Great Place to Work Institute's survey, the highest scoring companies are ranked, with the top 100 being deemed to be the best to work for. Specifically, it is about how the leadership of a company creates an environment whereby employees at all levels identify strongly with and score highly when benchmarked against the Great Place to Work Institute's Trust Index survey of staff and the Culture Audit of management. Collectively, they directly relate to management and staff acting and being seen to act with heightened integrity.

Edmans (2012) provides in his article a cross section of the Institute's proprietary questions of management and statements for staff.

The Group would probably achieve a very high rating in terms of the following:

- How do you inspire employees to feel that their work has more meaning than being 'just a job'?
- What are the distinctive ways in which management… shares information… with employees?
- What avenues are available for employees to communicate with management?
- Management keeps me informed about important issues and changes.
- I can ask management any reasonable question and get a straight answer.

- This is a psychologically and emotionally healthy place to work.
- Management shows a sincere interest in me as a person, not just as an employee.
- I'm proud to tell others I work here.
- When you join the company, you are made to feel welcome.

For a minority of questions and statements, the Group's rating would probably be medium as it is work in progress with room for improvement:

- How does your company show appreciation and/or recognition for employees' good work and extra effort?
- Please describe any special or unique benefits/perks that you offer.
- In what ways does your company celebrate its successes?
- Everyone has an opportunity to get special recognition.
- This is a fun place to work.

There is only one area where the Group would probably score a low rating; for staff in response to the statement '*I feel I receive a fair share of the profits made by this organisation*'. It would probably be very unusual for staff in many companies to respond with a high rating that they feel that they do get a fair share of their company profits.

The Group is changed dramatically. It is transformed. An exceptional workplace quality is established in the company with an embedded culture of heightened integrity:

- Its leaders create an atmosphere where they have credibility from their people that they listen, care and are inspiring. Its leaders are predominantly consistent, disciplined and transparent in their policies, processes and actions.
- There is a shift from having a highly negative and dysfunctional culture with declining profits in a growing market, to being a recognised world leader, delivering superior profits with evident traction for more growth. This is through a highly positive culture shaped and driven by its purpose. Risk aversion is overtaken by a growth mindset.
- At its heart, its leaders and its people enjoy a very high level of mutual trust and confidence. Its people are highly motivated because they have greater accountability, competence and empowerment to bring up problems and resolve them themselves within a practical set of ethical guidelines. Employees now believe that they are treated with respect and fairness.

In brief, the Group moves substantially towards being '*a great place to work*'.

It also fulfils to a significant extent the attributes set out by Blueprint for Better Business's (2017) framework for defining purpose: It requires that each person is a someone, not a something and that a company must value and treat its people with dignity. Where these attributes of purpose are clearly evident in a company, then it must be a great place to work.

Purpose: Measurable Business Payoffs

The Big Innovation Centre (2016) sets out nine measurable business payoffs that should be expected from a company that is led and operated with purpose. The metrics are superior share price performance; improved accounting and operational performance; lower cost of capital; more valuable innovation; improved recruitment, retention and motivation of employees; less adversarial industrial relations; larger firm size and decentralisation; smaller regulatory fines; and greater resilience in the face of external shocks. The measures are based on a systematic review of the literature which cumulatively provides impressive empirical support for these business outcomes:

- Superior share price performance: As the Group is privately owned by a private equity house, share price performance can be equated to the sales multiple of EBITDA[1] profits achieved on exit. It is sold at a premium of 20 per cent to the prevailing market rate.
- Improved accounting and operational performance:

  - Cash conversion (defined as cash flow realised from operations as a percentage of EBITDA) is consistently high at 85 per cent, even after capital expenditure. Board papers with full financial and other reports are available within eight working days of the month end, with flash financial results (which consolidated the financial results from all country corporate entities) being available within five working days of the month end.
  - Staff productivity increases substantially; revenue contribution per employee increases by 42 per cent; EBITDA profit per employee increases by 67 per cent; and return on sales increases nearly threefold over the seven years.
  - As all investment is funded through retained earnings, the Group enjoys a 'lower cost of capital' than if debt has been raised from the market. Tangible and intangible investment in technology, R&D, country offices, apprenticeships and the training centre are the equivalent of an annual run rate of circa 25 per cent of year one profits.

- More valuable innovation: This is readily evident for its investment in R&D and hence new innovative products being released. As reported earlier:

  - For the marine sector, a dominant market share is achieved.
  - For the power sector, the burner is classified in the US as the 'latest best technology'.
  - For the process sector, a continental European client describes the new burner at a major international conference as the 'best in the world'.
  - The average value of contracts doubles in size.

In terms of intangible investment and results, the internet-based 'Knowledge Bank' is acclaimed as an industry first by a prospective multinational buyer of the Group, in enabling all staff irrespective of their location in the world to have full access to core proprietary data and information.

- Improved recruitment, retention and motivation of employees: Staff turnover decreases threefold over three years and becomes a third of the level of the UK industry level staff turnover, which indicated that motivation has increased substantially. Staff absenteeism remains low. Reduced staff absenteeism and turnover result in an annual saving and improved cash flow equivalent to 20 per cent of year one profits. These cost savings, as increased profits, generate a seven per cent point increase in the subsequent sale price achieved for the Group.

Motivation of staff and staff satisfaction are extremely high due to a combination of improvements in staff terms and conditions, the face-to-face and interactive engagement of communications, and the reporting of action taken in response to staff satisfaction surveys and workshop sessions. In year six in the UK, the Group is awarded 'Investor in People' status at its first attempt.

- Larger firm size and decentralisation: Revenue increases by 200 per cent and staff numbers by 85 per cent over the seven years. Decentralisation is clearly evident with an additional seven country offices being opened within the first four years to 19 countries in total, and, importantly in terms of how they operate, as exemplified by the company's Knowledge Bank which provides all employees with unfettered access to over 80 per cent of data and information held by the Group.

- Less adversarial industrial relations: There is a fundamental shift from the first two years when negotiations with trade unions about annual salary increments break down, to later years when the trade unions support substantial restructuring of the Group and changes in its pension scheme.
- Smaller regulatory fines: The Group continues its excellent track record of zero regulatory, environmental and health and safety incidents and no fines. It not only complies with transfer pricing requirement but also does not practice tax avoidance.
- Resilience in the face of external shocks: It continues to deliver above budgeted financial results during and after three failed sales processes (two of which are of the company itself and one is of its private equity owners). This is also in the face of the unexpected resignation of two board executive directors; and a major litigation resolution which could have bankrupted the Group.

In addition, a purpose-defined company could be expected to deliver excellent customer service:

- As reported earlier, the Group's quality of customer service is assessed in detail as part of two sets of commercial due diligence conducted by a specialist market research company.[2] In the earlier survey, the level of customer satisfaction is exceedingly poor. There are a considerable number of issues and dissatisfied customers. Three years later in the subsequent survey, there is not one dissatisfied customer and the quality of customer satisfaction is rated as excellent.

Wider Applicability of the Model

The successful benchmarking against best practice provides powerful evidence-based argument that it is almost axiomatic that when a purpose-defined company is being led and operated with heightened integrity (as a core business process), then its open and transparent culture can largely be defined in terms of Blueprint for Better Business's five behavioural principles.

The case study multinational corporation is demonstrated as being a responsible and responsive employer, being honest and fair with its customers and suppliers, being a guardian of the environment for future generations, and being a good citizen.[3] It is a '*great place to work*' in terms of the defining attributes of the Great Place to Work Institute. And, when the case study's results are benchmarked against The Big Innovation Centre's nine measurable business payoffs expected from a purpose-defined company, the Group's performance is also in accordance with these exacting requirements for being a purpose company.

Nevertheless, it is unlikely that one size fits all for the actual delivery of a company's defined purpose. Whilst the successful benchmarking of the core business process model against third-party best practice provides a high degree of confidence as to its wider validity beyond a single case study demonstration, it is nevertheless a highly prescriptive approach. Hence, it needs to be questioned as to which sectors or types of businesses the model is most likely to be applicable and equally those where it is unlikely to be applicable.

The 'Heightened Integrity Model' is highly relevant to where a company's people and its intangible assets are critical for delivery of its business and its purpose. Delivery of knowledge assets (such as ideas, patents, brands, software copyrights and the interrelationships a company has with its workforce, suppliers and customers) is critically dependent on the performance of a company's people. A classic example here is Unilever under its current CEO (Alan Jope) and its prior leader (Paul Polman) with its 155,000 staff and 400 brands being sold in 190 countries. And, intangible assets are growing to be much more important than tangible assets for many sectors (See Table 8.1).

At first sight, the model could appear to be less applicable to capital-intensive and large-scale activities such as oil and gas exploration and related upstream processing such as ethylene plants and LNG carriers. However, this is not the case. It is highly appropriate for such activities.

An example here is BP under John Browne's regime as its chairman and CEO. The company is strongly criticised for its poor management and cost-cutting policy in relation to its maintenance and safety (*The Week* 2010; Hazards 2015). When maintenance and safety regimes prove to be inadequate for large-scale capital-intensive activities, they can have a hugely disproportionate impact: Explosions with catastrophic damage to the capital-intensive facilities, with often related disastrous pollution and loss of lives.

For example, in the Gulf of Mexico Deepwater Horizon oil spill in 2010 (the largest oil spill then to date), 11 people are killed with billions of US dollars of costs being incurred for environmental clean-up, compensation and fines. It can be argued that for certain members of the consortium of companies:

- If their leaders *demonstrated the right moral tone from the top*, then design, construction, operation, maintenance and safety would not have been compromised as a cost-saving initiative.

- And, if their staff are *radically engaged and communicated with*, then they would have been empowered to raise their concerns most strongly about such cost savings.
- And, if the *feedback loop between the leaders and their people is closed*, then their concerns would have reached their leaders who would then have taken, and would have been seen to have taken, the appropriate corrective action.

This illustrates that a company's *people are the connection that matters* in capital-intensive industries due to the huge and disproportionate importance of design, construction, operation, maintenance and safety policies and practices. Where there are inadequacies in their actual delivery, this would abnegate a company's defined purpose. And, if there is an *'ethos of integrity and compliance embodied'* in the company, then the issues would be raised and resolved before any catastrophic disaster with ensuing pollution and loss of lives.

That is, if companies in large-scale, capital-intensive activities adopt the 'Heightened Integrity Model' to deliver their company's defined purpose, then their people 'at the shop floor' would be empowered with the responsibility and accountability to require its leaders to redress inadequacies in policy regimes that prejudice their company's defined purpose and company leaders would have responded.

With respect to 'Tech titans' (such as Amazon, Apple, Google and Facebook) and their reportedly anti-competitive practices, a legislative response would probably require them to move to become purposeful. Nevertheless, in principle, there are no major reasons for why the core business process model, as the basis for leading and operating a company by heightened integrity to deliver its defined purpose, would not be applicable. For such companies, their people are the intangible asset and stakeholders that matter for delivering their performance. More than 20,000 Google employees globally staged a walk out in protest at its plans for a censored Chinese version of its search engineer, which it subsequently abandoned.

Overall, the successful benchmarking against independent third-party best practice also serves to demonstrate the wider applicability of the model. They are based on a considerable amount of survey evidence from a wide range of companies encompassing all sectors of business activity.

The challenge outstanding is whether the 'Heightened Integrity Model' also meets the pivotal requirement that when implemented by a purpose-led company, long-term sustainable performance for the economy and society is delivered (i.e. Blueprint for Better Business's first principle of a purpose-driven company).

Notes

1 EBITDA: Earnings before interest, tax, depreciation and amortisation.
2 AMR International Ltd is a professional services firm that conducts commercial due diligence assessments.
3 It should be acknowledged that A Blueprint for Better Business's (2016) requirements underpinning its five principles are more comprehensive than those demonstrated by the selected aspects of the case study company's practices. However, only a small cross section of examples from the case study company have been presented.

References

A Blueprint for Better Business (2016). "*Purpose and performance: The benefits of following the five principles of a purpose driven business*". A Blueprint for Better Business. London.
A Blueprint for Better Business (2017). *ibid*.
Edmans, A. (2012). *ibid*.
Hazards (2015) 'Safe hands?', 122, April–June, http://www.hazards.org/oil. Accessed 20 April 2016.
The Big Innovation Centre (2016). *ibid*.
The Week (2010) 'BP "flouted safety regs on North Sea platform"', 15 September, http://www.theweek.co.uk. Accessed 20 April 2016.

Chapter 7

DELIVERED

Bigger Benefits for Society and Bigger Profits for Business

The Group's challenging and ambitious purpose is defined as follows:

- We contribute to a healthier environment for society and become a guardian of the environment for future generations.
- We benefit society with products and services that result in cleaner air and reduced depletion of natural resources in a long-term sustainable manner.
- We provide technical solutions for reducing the adverse environmental impact of companies operating predominantly in the global, dynamic and generally noxious downstream oil and gas sectors.
- We deliver world-leading, cost-effective combustion burners and related services to reduce emissions and increase fuel efficiency with absolute safety.

That is, the Group has a purpose that is in full accordance with Blueprint for Better Business' prime principle for defining a purpose company: It delivers long-term sustainable performance.

Delivery by the Group of long-term sustainable performance is readily demonstrated by calling on the integrated business reporting taxonomy of types of capital that comprise a company's activities. They serve to balance and integrate delivery of a company's purpose in terms of natural, intellectual, human, social and financial capital returns.

With respect to natural capital, the starting point for the Group is to ensure it offers a product range that reduces emissions with greater fuel efficiency and absolute safety.

- *Natural capital*: Reduced depletion of natural resources and a healthier environment[1]:

    - Reduced emissions/pollution; cleaner air.
    - Greater fuel efficiency; reduced use of fossil fuels.
    - Greater safety; fewer polluting disasters.

Previously: Aided and abetted depletion.

For intellectual capital, the Group must deliver world-leading products and, importantly, deliver on business intangibles so that synergies are achieved, whereby the whole is greater than the sum of the individual parts.

- *Intellectual capital*: World-leading technical and operational performance of products at competitive prices:

    - Emissions reduction.
    - Greater fuel efficiency.
    - Absolute safety.

    and
    business intangibles/synergies delivered:

    - Collaboration across business units, functions and geographies
    - Work seamlessly delivered across organisational boundaries.

    Previously: Minimal.

The Group's people are the stakeholder connection that matters for delivery of its purpose in practical terms.

- *Human capital*: Empowered:

    - Staff: Meaningful work, high self-worth, fulfilled and emotionally committed.
    - Reduced mismanagement and maladministration.
    - Alignment of stakeholders to a common purpose agenda.

    Previously: Dysfunctional culture.

In being led and operated with heightened integrity as the hub of the core business process model, this delivers its social capital.

- *Social capital*: Greater market efficiency and allocation of resources:

    - Stronger governance.
    - Reduced non-compliance.
    - Regulatory traction:
        - No tax evasion.
        - No systemic tax avoidance.
        - No gaming of regimes.
        - Surpassing product technical requirements.
    - Honest and fair treatment of suppliers and customers throughout its supply chain.
    - No corruption.

    Previously: Declining social capital.

As profits follow and result from successful delivery of the Group's defined purpose, then its financial capital also benefits.

- *Financial capital*: Substantial shareholder returns:
  - Superior profitability:
    - 18 per cent cagr[2] EBITDA,
    - revenue growing at 12 per cent pa in a market growing at 7 per cent pa.
  - High cash conversion: 85 per cent.
  - Premium sale value: 20 per cent.

  Previously: Decreasing returns.

The case study company's purpose is seen to benefit all stakeholders: shareholders, employees, customers, suppliers, communities, the environment and the economy in a longer-term sustainable manner.

It is useful to challenge and question whether it is the core business process model of leading and operating with heightened integrity that delivers the bigger benefits for society and bigger profits for the Group:

- Or, is it a classic transformational corporate change programme of, for example, stretch targets, inclusiveness for buy-in, an empowered organisation to deliver, inherent pride to generate the right culture, well-designed processes for implementation of details of change and tracking of progress, and alignment of incentives to meet corporate goals?
- Or, is it the result of considerable investment in R&D facilities and hence new products; the opening and growth of additional country offices, training facilities, financial systems, internet-based data system, new products, growth of spares and service, people, communications and so on?
- Or, is it a fortuitous combination of factors, such as a growing market, dormant competitors, aggressive private equity owners, a good CEO and luck?
- Or, would there be success if the Group operates in a declining market?

It must also be recognised that delivery of the Group's defined purpose involves a number of necessary but not sufficient factors:

- A first-class top team that consistently delivers results that exceed the challenging double-digit growth budgets.
- Making the most of unexpected opportunities, which the CEO takes full advantage of and which provide the basis for a significant business turnaround in the first year.

- Developing and delivering a portfolio business model and two-game strategy, which provide considerable upside and little downside risk for the business.
- Taking market share from competitors in a growing market due to significant investment.
- Substantial investment in R&D which delivers market-leading and price-competitive new products.
- Investment in country offices which result in a stronger global distribution network.
- The private equity house owners providing continuous positive support.

The critical success factor is the proactive and relentless commitment of leading and operating the Group with a culture of heightened integrity:

- It is how the corporate transformation programme is implemented.
- It is at the hub of the Group relentlessly pursuing its defined purpose.
- It pervades the entire organisation in the entirety of how it did what it did.

That is, the application of the 'Heightened Integrity Model' to the case study company demonstrates with evidence-based argument the *'How'* to deliver a company's defined purpose.

The Group does benefit society with products and services that result in cleaner air and reduced depletion of natural resources in a long-term sustainable manner. Delivery of its purpose does directly contribute to a healthier environment for society, thereby illustrating how social and environmental outcomes link back directly to a company's purpose. And, for its shareholders, superior financial returns are made. Both society and the Group are better off from delivery of its purpose.

Notes

1 Many of the outcomes are largely internal metrics with the extent to which society has been served (i.e. parts of social and natural capital) being but two of the five metrics. Additionally, there has been no measurement of their impact. In hindsight, it would have been practical to record the expected savings in emissions and fuel efficiency for each new contract through comparing installation performance against the next-best technology alternative or prior installation performance.
2 cagr: compound average growth rate.

Chapter 8

RECONNECTING

A Growing Range of Programmes and Legislation for Reconnecting Business with Society

There is now a sea change in attitude towards the primacy of purpose over the prior decades of focusing on the primacy of shareholder value. Evidence of this is the increasing number of very different purpose-driven programmes and legislation that are underway with the objective of re-connecting business with society.

Believer Companies

There are some 'believer' companies, such as Unilever and GSK in the UK, which are pioneering the delivery of being, and being seen to be, a purpose-driven company in a long-term sustainable manner. In addition, a number of companies, such as the RSB banking group, are working closely with Blueprint for Better Business to become purpose-driven companies.

In addition to a board and its chairperson establishing a company's purpose, believer companies require a believer CEO with the ambition and mindset or psyche who wants to lead the creation and maintenance of a corporation based on a pro-integrity approach to business life. This goes beyond relishing the challenge of leading a successful business. It must also include being instrumental in setting, committing and delivering the intrinsic challenge of leading a company based on a bold pro-integrity ethos to deliver the board's defined company purpose.

Believer Proclaimers

An innovative development originating in the US is the formation of 'Benefit Corporations'. Benefit Corporations enshrine in their articles of association that in addition to their commercial objectives of making a profit, they have a fiduciary duty or public purpose not only to shareholders but also to major stakeholders. This encompasses serving the interests of workers, customers, suppliers, the community and the environment. Legislation requires annual benefit reports to be publicly available. The directors of Benefit Corporations are legally required to discharge these objectives. Failure to do so can result in shareholders taking legal recourse for them to do so.

A benefit company does not have to be certified by a third party. However, B Lab (a not-for-profit organisation) sets out a comprehensive third-party standard covering 15 goals a company must fulfil to be certified as a benefit company by B Lab. By early 2020, around 3,250 companies across 71 countries have been certified by B Lab.

Early in 2020, the UK sees the launch of the 'Good Business Charter', by an independent not-for-profit organisation, to promote responsible business. Its charter measures company behaviour over ten components (which broadly align to Blueprint for Better Business' five principles). Companies achieve accreditation when they meet all ten commitments. By mid-2020, there are some 100 companies in the UK which are signed up to the charter and are accredited.

In the US in August 2019, 181 CEOs belonging to the 'Business Roundtable' (BRT) publicly pledge to great acclaim to serve staff, suppliers, communities and customers as well as shareholders. However, subsequent analysis shows that only two of them (Duke Energy and Marriott) tie CEO bonuses to a quantified stakeholder metric with the majority still being driven by shareholder value. In addition, 70 per cent of the BRT signatories are incorporated in Delaware and their hands might be tied as the state's corporate law requires that directors must make stockholder welfare their sole aim, according to a statement by the state's former chief justice (Bebchuk and Tallarita 2020).

Some companies may be subscribing to such initiatives and gaming the reporting metrics as part of creating a good public image, whilst others will be practising and demonstrating their purpose. An independent third-party assessment of the extent to which such schemes actually lead to companies being more purposeful would provide greater clarity as to the actual extent to which subscriber companies are indeed purposeful.

Believer Investors

Some major private investors are rising to the challenge of requiring target and owned firms to adopt a purpose-driven agenda. Larry Fink, chief executive, BlackRock (a global investment fund) in his 2018 letter to CEOs states that a company should: "... *Make a positive contribution to society, not just deliver profit... (be a) good employer as a long-term strategy... (with) regular interrogation of management practices...*". However, actual delivery of business purpose of corporations owned by 'believer investors' will nevertheless require believer chairpersons and CEOs.

For believer companies, investors and proclaimers, the coronavirus pandemic of 2020 and subsequent economic recession will help to demonstrate the extent to which they have acted in practice under the stresses of unprecedented adverse business and economic circumstances (in sharp contrast to the bull market of the past decade or so). It would show whether they are mere purpose proclaimers rather than actual purpose practitioners.

Purpose-Based Legislation

In the UK, there are legislative changes to corporate reporting requirements. With effect from January 2019, amendments were made to Section 172(1) of the Companies Act of 2006 and the Financial Reporting Council's (FRC) reporting requirements; with both having the same broad objective. It is one of moving companies from a narrow objective of maximising shareholder returns to one of taking into account other stakeholders. They now include an explicit purpose-based agenda.

Under Section 172(1) of the Companies Act, "*Duty to promote the success of the company*", the new reporting requirements include having regard for stakeholders in terms of "*... the interests of employees ... foster relationships with suppliers, customers and others ... impact of operations on the community and the environment...*". This applies to all companies with turnover above £36m, balance sheet assets above £18m and with more than 250 employees. However, it is essentially toothless in terms of enforcement. A board has only to demonstrate that it takes the concern of its stakeholders into account in arriving at its decision. There is little recourse from disadvantaged stakeholders. This is because the key tenet of the 2006 Companies Act remains unchanged: Company directors are solely accountable to their members or shareholders.

With respect to the FRC's new code of corporate reporting that premium listed companies must follow, it includes the requirements: "*...to assess and monitor alignment of culture with the purpose, values and strategy of the company ... preserve value over the long term ... and have engaged with their workers...*". The FRC is increasingly and closely scrutinising the behavioral aspects of how a company's defined purpose is manifested in practice. In late 2020, the FRC conducted a "*Review of Compliance Reporting*" (2020). Its main finding is that companies are predominantly reporting is formulaic box-ticking compliance, which is totally counter to the stated intention of the legislation.

The FRC expects to receive further powers concerning the quality of company reporting and it intends to call out poor compliance. In addition to requiring boards to have a well-defined purpose statement and then to demonstrate progress in achieving it, the FRC's expectations appear to be more precise and prescriptive. This extends beyond how the board reaches key decisions and their impact. It requires the setting out of initiatives with greater clarity and measurement of their performance or impact (on, such as, culture, diversity, executive remuneration, engagement with and understanding key stakeholders) along with details of steps taken, methods, processes and metrics used and on how feedback is being taken into account. That is, the FRC is focussing on how a company behaves in delivering its defined purpose. It is largely in behavioural terms that resonate greatly with Millennials' values and beliefs.

It could be argued that as there is a clear and growing body of evidence that purpose-driven companies financially outperform other companies, it would be in the self-enlightened interest of boards, their chairpersons and CEOs to define and implement a purpose-driven strategy. And, as such, there is then no need for legislation setting out compulsory requirements. Such a view however fails to recognise that many shareholders can be benign: with their boards and/or their chairpersons and/or their CEOs being 'satisficers' rather than 'maximisers' with respect to purpose and related financial performance.

Third-Party Assessment and Ranking

An unexplored initiative is third-party assessment and ranking of the purposefulness of corporations. If conducted in the UK for say major FTSE corporations (say the FTSE 100 and 250 corporations), such scrutiny would be of significant public interest. It would show the relative extent to which these major corporations are being led and operate as purpose companies. What is being suggested here is similar to Transparency International's annual league table that ranks countries by an index of their perceived level of corruption.

The information sources could be corporations' annual reports and their annual submission to the Financial Reporting Council and media reports. Both of these statutory information sources are in the public domain and, as noted above, have reporting requirements relating to stakeholder purpose and returns. This would give the required consistency of corporation-specific information sources for the proposed ranking. In addition, there is a need to take into account any 'bad' behaviour in a particular year that has not been reported by a corporation in its statutory returns. As such behaviour could resonate for several years, a say three-year rolling average for corporations' annual rank would facilitate taking such 'bad' behaviour into account. Corporations' 'purpose' attributes and practices could then be assessed and 'scored' by benchmarking them against the five principles of a purpose-driven business put forward by Blueprint for Better Business and The Big Innovation Centre's nine measurable business payoffs of a purpose company. A three-year composite score could then be calculated to arrive at the 'Corporate Purpose Ranking Index'.

Strong performers on the ranking would deserve praise and weak ones would probably receive public shaming.

With widespread publicity, such a high-profile publicly available ranking of major corporations could impact their branding and reputation, especially with Millennials and Generation Z, both positively and negatively. This could be very powerful, given the value that Millennial and Generation Z reportedly place on whether they are working for a purpose-driven corporation. As summarised by Edmans (2020):

- The PwC/AIESEC study... concluded that "millennials want to be proud of their employer, to feel that their company's value match their own, and that the work they do is worthwhile". In a Deloitte survey, only 27 per cent of millennials responded that "they intend to stay with their current employer for five years, but 88 per cent said that they would do so if they were satisfied with the company sense of purpose". The stakes are high.
- Gallup "estimated that millennial turnover due to lack of engagement costs US economy over $30 billion dollars per year" (page 193).

For laggards in the 'Corporate Purpose Ranking Index', their poor ranking could 'name-and-shame' their often-reticent shareholders, chairpersons and non-executive directors to act with greater alacrity in holding their corporations to account and thereby adopt a more purpose-driven corporate agenda.

With success, the 'Corporate Purpose Ranking Index' could be expanded internationally with establishment of say a US Fortune 500 purpose ranking index.

A challenge as ever is the extent to which some corporations would seek to game the purposefulness performance metrics. They could focus on managing the metrics rather than being more purposeful. And some parties would challenge the adoption of Blueprint for Better Business' five principles of a purpose-driven business and The Big Innovation Centre's nine measurable business payoffs of a purpose company for such a ranking exercise as there is no general agreement on how to measure a company's purpose.

The greater the extent to which these programmes and policies are mutually reinforcing, the greater the chance of success of business reconnecting with society.

Company Purpose: Root Cause and Leadership

There are two long-term trends that could shift company purpose from being a 'nice-to-have' to one of becoming an inescapable and inevitable requirement for business. They are:

- The intergenerational shift in values and beliefs between the 'Baby Boomers' of the 1980s / 90s and the 'Millennials' of the 2000s onwards.
- The shift in the basis of company investment valuation over broadly the same periods.

The two trends are increasingly entwined (Figure 8.1). They are symbiotic. They are the root cause of the 'Company purpose' agenda.

During the 1980s /1990s, the Baby Boomers generation (born c.1946–1964, age c.57–75 years old) overthrew the deferential, hierarchical values of their parents. They replaced them with libertarian, rights-of-the-individual values. Their personal characteristics can be summarised as: Strong work ethic, self-assured, independent, competitive, goal-centric, resourceful, mentally focused, team oriented and disciplined. They communicate largely by face to face meetings and by telephone. Their main media are TV and newspapers.

A fundamental libertarian belief of the Baby Boomer generation is one of companies maximising shareholder value; as promulgated by Milton Friedman's free market capitalism.

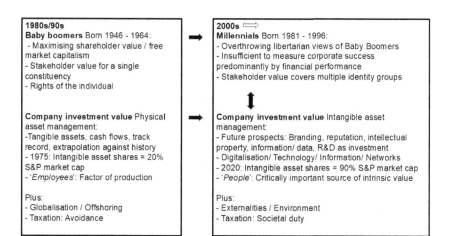

Figure 8.1 Purpose Company: Root Cause.

During this same period of the 1980s /1990s, company value investment is assessed largely in terms of physical asset management of tangible assets, cash flow, track record and essentially extrapolation against previous performance. The value of tangible assets on company balance sheet are pledged with equity against debt. That is, corporate leverage is a function of debt against a company's tangible assets. This is a period of globalisation and offshoring, and taxation avoidance.

Here, a company's 'Employees' are one of the factors of production. A company's culture is shaped by the corporate drive of maximising shareholder value.

For the period 2000s onwards, Millennials (born c.1981–1996, c.25–40 years old) become a global majority losing faith in democracy and its institutions compared to their parents and grandparents when at the same stage of life. They think differently, act differently and have different values. They are the largest single group eligible to vote in many OECD countries. Their wealth is growing. They have an accentuated concern about the cause of environmental issues and their resolution. By 2025, they form 75% of the world's workforce.

Their personal characteristics can be summarised as: Confident, ambitious and achievement-oriented. They have high expectations of their employers; tend to seek new challenges at work; and, are not afraid to question authority. They love their phones with texting and similar applications being the preferred form of communication. Their main means of communication is via virtual communities. Media sources are predominantly online.

And similarly, from around the 2000s onwards company value investment is increasingly assessed in terms of the future value of intangible assets. That is: Branding, reputation, patents, other intellectual property, information / data and R & D as investment. It is a period characterised by digitalisation, technology, information and where network effects are paramount. There is also an increasing concern about companies' externalities and their adverse impact on the environment. The shifting of tangible assets to locations off-balance sheet has accelerated. Hard assets such as land, property and plant are now held by special purpose vehicles and owned by third parties and leased or 'rented'. Off-balance sheet assets / items are no longer a factor of production but a service available for production. In terms of the balance of the S & P 500 market cap between intangible and tangible assets, 90% of it is in intangibles by 2020; as compared to 20% in 1975 (Cembalest, 2020). This is a period of externalities and concern about adverse environmental issues. Taxation is now often seen as a societal duty.

That is, over the periods of the 1980s / 90s and 2000 onwards, company investment valuation has shifted dramatically from physical assets to intangible assets; and, from employees as a factor of production to a company's people as intrinsic value creators.

Now, a company's 'People' are the fundamental source of creating company investment value.

Millennials believe that it is insufficient to measure company success predominantly by financial performance. They are in the driving seat and are gaining political and economic traction by replacing Baby Boomers in shaping the dominant values in society. Millennials are challenging libertarian values and replacing them with rights-of-the-identity-group values; where stakeholder value encompasses multiple identity groups. This, in turn, requires a new core competence whereby a company's culture results in it being led and operated on a higher ethical plain i.e. with heightened integrity.

A prime example here is the experience of Google and its people. Its people are its prime asset for the definition and delivery of its technology platform. In 2018, Google is developing a search app for the Chinese market: 'Project Dragonfly'. Google employees publish an open letter protesting against the search engine as it would help the Chinese government to extend its already extensive surveillance state. Lack of action by Google leads to highly co-ordinated demonstration by some 20,000 employees outside its offices worldwide. Amid such visible and adverse feedback from its people, Google subsequently cancels Project Dragonfly. Google's people can be seen to be demanding primacy of purpose they value over primacy of shareholder value. Given Google's critical dependence on them as the foundation and source of its intangible assets, it had to respond accordingly.

Moreover, as noted above, Millennials reportedly place a very high value on whether they are working for a purpose - driven company. This has a direct impact on companies' employee attraction and retention (e.g. 85% of young leaders agree or strongly agree that business success in the 21st century will be re-defined by more than just profit). And, Millennials want to be proud of their employer, to feel that their company's values match their own, and that the work they do is worthwhile (e.g. whilst two out of three millennials expect to leave their current company within five years, nearly 90% also said that they are likely to stay longer if they are satisfied with their company's sense of purpose).

That is, with many companies being dependent on intangible assets as their source of investment value, it becomes an inescapable prerequisite for them to operate on a higher ethical plane and related moral compass if they wish to attract, retain and motivate their fundamental and highly mobile source of intrinsic value: their people.

It then becomes axiomatic that delivery of a company's purpose requires it to be led and operated by its CEO with a culture of heightened integrity. It is a major source of competitive advantage and business success.

References

Aldwinckle, R. (2019). *"Piffle or pertinent: Does your company have a purpose?"*. A Blueprint for Better Business. London.

Bebchuk, L. and Tallarita, R. (2020). *"Going in circles"*. Cited in The Economist, 14 March, page 58.

Cembalest, M. (2020). *"Eye on the market 2021 Outlook"*. J P Morgan.

Edmans, A. (2020). *ibid*.

FRC (2020). "Review of Corporate Governance".frc.org.uk

Fink, L. (2018). *ibid*.

Chapter 9

RESOLUTION
For Society, and for a Company

Capitalism itself is increasingly realising that it is in crisis. But capitalism will not heal itself. Action is needed at the society level and at the company level for business to reconnect with society.

For Society

For reconnecting business with society, no big bang resolution is expected. There is not a single magic bullet to bring about the much-needed reconnection between business and society. It will be incremental. In practical terms, incremental change through a diverse portfolio of programmes and legislation, collectively and over time, results in increasing companies' primacy of purpose.[1]

Primacy of shareholder value has been entrenched in company stakeholders' mindsets for many, many decades. A change requires a paradigm shift to primacy of purpose. Adding further complexity to the required huge shift of focus for companies is their highly heterogeneous nature, and the equally highly heterogeneous nature of their CEOs, chairpersons, boards, shareholders and other stakeholders.

Reconnecting business with society is decidedly on the corporate and public agenda. Whilst each of the programmes and legislation summarised in Chapter 8 have advantages and limitations, they would individually and collectively result in varying degrees of increased purposefulness of companies.

In certain respects, each or any combination of them could be viewed as nudging a company's board and/or its chairperson and/or its CEO to bring about greater purposefulness in their company's business activities. For example, the Behavioural Insights Team (2015) – also known as the 'Nudge Unit' and formerly part of the UK government's Cabinet Office – has reportedly achieved considerable successful outcomes in altering people's behaviour by making small changes. Drawing on behavioural science expertise, it examines closely how people make choices about the actions they take in response to a wide variety of government policies that require direct interaction with individuals. It uses nudge techniques that play on reciprocity and personal choice in order to nudge people into making choices that lead to better lives.

Just as individuals can be nudged to change their behaviour so too could chairpersons and CEOs of companies in response to some combination of the push of policies and/or the pull of programmes outlined above for reconnecting business with society. That is, different types of companies, boards, chairpersons and CEOs can be expected to respond to or be nudged differently by different types of policies and/or programmes. Some will be pulled as 'believers', others will need to be pushed by legislation or by being 'shamed' in having a low public ranking of purposefulness. No one size will fit all in delivering the purpose agenda. A portfolio of purpose policies and programmes is required and recommended.

Whichever policies or programmes result in changing the mindset of a board, chairperson or CEO to adopt pursuit of a purpose-defined agenda, company purpose needs to be delivered in practical terms. As has been demonstrated earlier, there is a considerable body of evidence-based guidance on the '*What*' to do to be a purpose-defined company.

For a Company

For companies, the 'purpose' agenda is switching from the '*Why*' do it and the '*What*' to do, to the '*How*' to do it. For company stakeholders, boards, chairpersons and CEOs, an evidence-based core business process model for the '*How*' to deliver a purpose-defined company has been comprehensively demonstrated: The 'Heightened Integrity Model'.

In addition to the case study application of the model, it has been successfully benchmarked against third-party best practice expected of a purpose-driven company, namely:

- The 'behavioural principles' of Blueprint for Better Business (2017).
- The attributes of a 'great place to work' of the Great Place to Work Institute (Edmans 2012).
- The 'measurable business payoffs' of The Big Innovation Centre (2016).

This provides greater veracity for the core business process model; its application to the case study company; its wider applicability to companies generally; and hence its rigor.

The demonstration and verification of the 'Heightened Integrity Model' is ground breaking:

- In terms of monitoring and reviewing the performance of a company with respect to its purposefulness, a range of non-financial and financial metrics have been demonstrated by application to the case study corporation. They consist of Blueprint for Better Business' five behavioural principles and The Big innovation Centre's nine measurable business payoffs (see Box 9.1).

- This provides stakeholders, company boards, their chairpersons, their CEOs and other stakeholders a demonstrated balanced range of metrics for assessing the extent to which their company delivers its purpose.
- And, for non-believer companies, the metrics present a considered basis for third parties to assess the extent to which such companies are falling short in playing their part in resolving the crisis facing capitalism: the growing disconnect between business and society.
- Additionally, an evidence-based illustration of the application of integrated business reporting for a purpose-driven company is set out.

For a company with a defined purpose, a culture of leading and operating it with heightened integrity results in bigger benefits for society and bigger profits for business. It is doing good and not doing bad; it is growing the pie, not a zero-sum game; it provides goods that are good and services that serve; and it is operating at a high ethical plane.

The loop is now complete for company purpose. In addition to the 'Why' and the 'What', there is now a business model (defined, demonstrated and verified by evidence-based argument) on the 'How' to actually deliver a company's defined purpose: The 'Heightened Integrity Model'.

Business thus becomes a force for good for society. Inefficient markets become more efficient.

Box 9.1 Non-financial and Financial Metrics for Assessing a Company's Purposefulness

Blueprint for Better Business' five principles of a purpose-driven business:

- Having purpose which delivers long-term sustainable performance for the economy.
- Being a responsible and responsive employer.
- Being honest and fair with customers and suppliers.
- Being a guardian of the environment for future generations.
- Being a good citizen.

The Big Innovation Centre's nine measurable business payoffs expected from a purpose-defined company:

- Superior share price performance.
- Improved accounting and operational performance.

- Lower cost of capital.
- More valuable innovation.
- Improved recruitment, retention and motivation of employees.
- Less adversarial industrial relations.
- Larger firm size and decentralisation.
- Smaller regulatory fines.
- Greater resilience in the face of external shocks.

Full details are presented in Chapters 5 and 6.

Note

1 This does not seek to address the policy concerns of rectifying the under-performing UK economy, as set out by The Big Innovation Centre (2016) and Mayer (2018).

References

A Blueprint for Better Business (2017) *ibid*.
Behavioural Insights Team (2015) *'Update report'*, https://www.bi.team/publications/the-behavioural-insights-teams-update-report-2015-16/. Accessed 18 January 2017.
Edmans, A. (2012). *ibid*.
Mayer, C. (2018). *ibid*.
The Big Innovation Centre (2016). *ibid*.

The Group's Business Model

The Group's Purpose

The Group's purpose determines its business model. Its purpose is:

- To contribute to a healthier environment for society and become a guardian for future generations.
- To benefit society with products and services that result in cleaner air and reduced depletion of natural resources in a long-term sustainable manner.
- To provide technical solutions for reducing the adverse environmental impact of companies operating predominantly in the global, dynamic and generally noxious downstream oil and gas sectors.
- To deliver world-leading, cost-effective combustion burners and related services to reduce emissions and increase fuel efficiency with absolute safety for:
  - Downstream oil and gas companies in the flares, petrochemicals and the marine sectors.
  - Hot water and steam raising applications in the industrial, agriculture/food processing, power plants and the marine sectors.

In delivering the Group's purpose, its vision includes being a world-leading provider of proven combustion solutions through technical excellence and cost leadership. Its ambition is to double the size of the business and grow profits faster than revenue within five years.

The 'Heightened Integrity Model', as a core business process, delivers the Group's overall business model for the execution of its purpose, values and strategy.

The Group's Market Sectors and Growth Drivers

Figure A.1 provides an overview of the market sectors and their growth drivers of emissions reduction and fuel efficiency. Their key unifying element for success is having R&D expertise and facilities to deliver world-leading combustion burners and services that reduce emissions and increase fuel efficiency with absolute safety, as is required in order to deliver the Group's purpose.

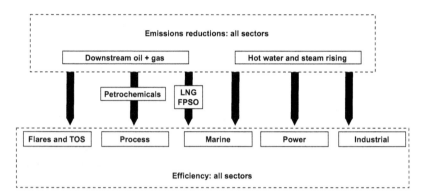

Figure A.1 Overview of the Group's market sectors and growth drivers

The Group's Complex Circumstances and Environment

In year one of the CEO being appointed, the Group faces a highly complex set of circumstances and environment for defining its purpose, vision and business model:

- R&D is not fit for purpose:
    - R&D is an inadequate core capability for new product sales for each of its five market sectors.
    - R&D infrastructure is predominantly aged with little recent investment.
    - Few new products have been released in recent years.
- Regulatory requirements are growing and diverse:
    - Increasing regulation is aimed at reduced emission requirements along with extensive health and safety legislation of the downstream oil and gas industry.

- Emission regulatory requirements vary from country to country.
- As the Group is a small player in its global marketplace and regulatory changes are nationally driven, it cannot expect to exert an influence on national regulatory authorities.
- The company operates at arm's length from the final customer and governments because its products form a relatively small part of very large engineering, procurement and construction contracts.

• Sales are predominantly international and highly diverse:

- Its domestic market is in decline and accounts for less than 15 per cent of annual sales.
- No major customers are consistently important from year to year.
- The top ten customers in a year account for less than 30 per cent of total annual sales.
- Membership of the top ten customers changes from year to year:
- It has five markedly different market sectors with little overlap of customers.
- No two main product sectors account for a majority of sales by value.
- It sells to over 80 countries.
- It has a wide range of routes to market: direct, through agents, through 100 per cent owned country offices and through two minority-owned joint ventures.
- Its capital product sales are via the intermediary and dominant party, engineering and procurement contractors (EPC) for multi-million-dollar plants.
- It rarely has a close direct relationship for capital product sales with the final end-user.
- Its bespoke products have to comply with being integrated into clients' often-huge installations.

• There is little inter-office coherence:

- They operate as discrete profit centres.
- They often view themselves as being in competition with each other as they dispute who should claim the ownership of sales and gross margin contribution.

• It has a highly negative culture:

- It is dysfunctional and having a lack of trust, secret side deals, little ambition.

- It is risk-averse with command-and-control hierarchical leadership.

- Its industrial sector is highly fragmented:

  - There is a large number of smaller companies which have well-established positions in their domestic market.
  - A small number of much larger companies have extensive international sales but are preoccupied with their large, vibrant domestic markets.
  - None of the larger companies enjoy a dominant market position in the Group's main market sectors.

Business Fundamentals for Positioning Delivery of the Group's Purpose and Vision

There are several business fundamentals for positioning the Group to deliver its purpose and vision:

- The Group has to have world-leading products in terms of their technical and operational performance (i.e. to reduce emissions and thereby leading to cleaner air; to increase fuel efficiency and thereby reduce the depletion of natural resources; and for absolute safety and thereby incurring fewer polluting incidents). There is a need for a fundamental overhaul of R&D in all of its aspects and for substantial capital investment at an unprecedented pace and scale.
- The Group has to have a much expanded and integrated network of offices for greater proximity to customers and providing excellent end-user after-sales customer service, thereby differentiating itself from its major competitors.
- To double the size of the business, it is necessary to have a range of both competitive and market-leading products and a wider and deeper geographical distribution network.
- For the Group's profits to grow faster than its revenue growth:

  - The gross margin contribution on its capital sales, spares and services sales has to grow.
  - There has to be disciplined control of costs and overheads which must grow slower than the increase in growth of revenues.

As summarised in Figure A.2, the Group's purpose and vision are at the centre and they drive and shape each of the fundamentals. Its purpose and vision are delivered via the core business process model of how the Group is led and operates – the 'Heightened Integrity Model'.

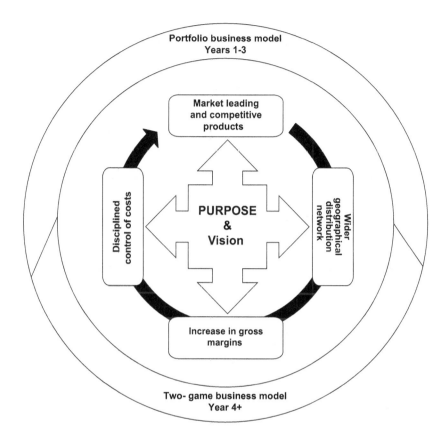

Figure A.2 Fundamentals for delivering the Group's purpose and vision

The Group's Portfolio Business Model

By the end of year one, the Group's portfolio business model and strategy have been formulated and have been communicated extensively with its people.

Its people know and understand that the Group has a diverse range of products, operates with country offices and agents, serves a disparate range of customers, has engineering and manufacturing facilities and outsources a lot of contracting.

With the benefit of substantial investment, this ad hoc mixture presents a highly diversified portfolio of revenue mix, great visibility of revenue and a series of different cash flows. Collectively, they provide the Group with strong business defensive qualities.

The portfolio business model consists of the following:

- Customer diversity, where in any one year, the top ten customers account for less than 30 per cent of total revenue.
- Five main product market sectors (Marine, Power, Process, Flares and Industrial applications), which have little overlap of customers and with each potentially contributing some 20 per cent of total sales.
- Four world regions (Europe, the Middle East, Asia Pacific and the Americas), which provide geographic market diversity and with each potentially contributing some 25 per cent of total sales per annum.
- Three distinct revenue sources (New products, Spares and Service), which have different gross margin contributions and cash flow profiles.

How it all fits together is illustrated in Figure A.3. The portfolio business model is brought to life and given practical meaning in communication sessions by the leadership team drawing an analogy of rotating parts of a Rubik's cube[1] to achieve the best combination of business advantages for the Group to deliver its purpose and strategy.

Towards the end of year three, many of the targets of the vision are being realised and delivery of its ambitious purpose is demonstrably evident. Its products and services result in lower emissions and less pollution, thereby contributing to a healthier environment. Its people have significant pride in working for the Group where its products directly lead to improvements in the environment to the benefit of society.

It is timely to reset the aspiration bar for the Group and to formulate a new business model: a two-game strategy. The revised stretch target is again to double the size of the business within five years and for profits to grow faster than revenue growth but through:

- *Game 1*: Continuing to do what the Group is good at, i.e. maintenance of the prime relationship with the intermediary EPC contractors (who specified and contracted the orders for new products).
- *Game 2*: Getting closer to and building up a stronger relationship with the facility end-user. This involves creating a series of wrap-around services in order to become a more embedded part of a customer's supply chain (see Figure A.4).

The wrap-around value-added services are mutually reinforcing from a customer perspective. They include customer burner tests at the R&D centre; long-term service contracts; technical training at the Group's training institute; turnkey contracts; site surveys of the operating regime

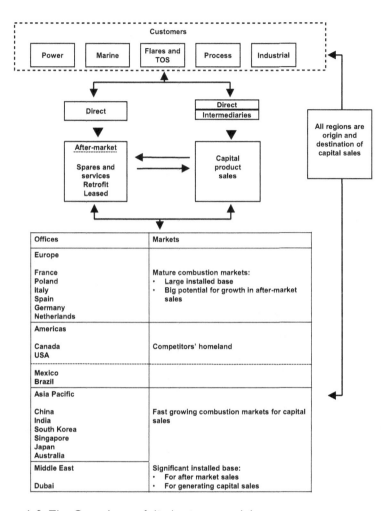

Figure A.3 The Group's portfolio business model

of installations; a 24/7 remote condition monitoring facility on burner systems; a global network of service engineers; and the establishment of a spares capability in each of its country offices.

The successful implementation of the purpose-driven portfolio business model with a two-game strategy provides a distinctive value proposition for customers that most competitors have difficulty in replicating. Few of them offer customers an integrated international network of offices with local spares and service capability in addition to an R&D programme of new product roll-out with market-leading edge performance in emissions reduction, cost savings and absolute safety. They provide

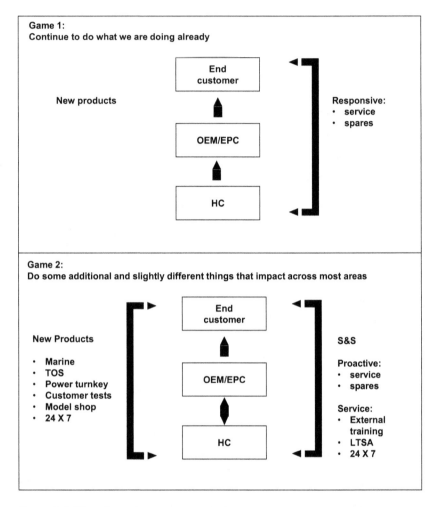

Figure A.4 The Group's two-game strategy

the foundation for delivery of the Group's purpose. The successful implementation of the core business process model, of leading and operating a company with heightened integrity, is the critical requirement for the actual delivery of the Group's defined purpose.

Note

1   The Rubik's Cube is a 3-D combination puzzle invented in 1974 by Hungarian sculptor and professor of architecture Ernő Rubik.

Index

Note: **Bold** page numbers refer to tables; *italic* page numbers refer to figures and page numbers followed by "n" denote endnotes.

accountability 33, 84; personal 14, 57
accounting performance 80
adversarial industrial relations 82
AMR International Ltd 85n2
apprenticeship programme 32, 33
autonomy 51, 53

Baby Boomers generation 5;
    fundamental libertarian belief of 95;
    libertarian beliefs 1
Behavioural Insights Team 99
beliefs: intergenerational shift in 95;
    values and 93
believer companies 90
believer investors 91–92
believer proclaimers 90–91
benchmarking 4, 13, 15, 56; against
    best practice 82; of core business
    process model 83; against five
    principles of purpose-driven
    business 93–94; against independent
    third-party best practice 84
Benefit Corporations 90–91
The Big Innovation Centre 7, 18, 56,
    83, 94, 102n1; corporate purpose
    12–13; defines company purpose
    8; interventionist leaning 12;
    measurable business payoffs 80–82;
    nine measurable business payoffs
    13, 101–102
B Lab 91
BlackRock 91
Blueprint for Better Business 7,
    18, 31, 56, 66, 76, 85n3, 90, 94;
    defines company purpose 8–9, 56;

five principles of purpose-driven
    business 17, 101; framework for
    defining purpose 79–80; legislative
    framework 14; principles of
    purpose-driven company 12;
    purpose-led to live and deliver 14
Browne, John 83
business: compliance-driven business
    33; core business process model
    15–16, 18, 22, 24, 28, 36, 56;
    evidence-based business model
    2, 17; integrity embody and
    compliance ethos in 33–36, **35–36**;
    measurable business payoffs
    80–82; portfolio business model
    107–110, *109, 110*; profits for
    86–89; pro-integrity business model
    52; purpose-driven business, five
    principles of 101; purpose-driven
    portfolio business model 109–110;
    reconnecting with society 99
business capital, category of 4
business outcomes 80–82
business performance 19
business process model 2
Business Roundtable (BRT) 91

capitalism 1, 12, 99
case study corporation 26–28
case study multinational corporation
    82–83
cash conversion 80
CEOs 2, 5, 15; behaviour and
    decisions 36; challenge for 21;
    in country offices closure 63–66;

formal interaction across Group 42, 43; Hamworthy Combustion Group 26–28; heightened integrity 20; Heightened Integrity Model 22; interaction between middle management and Group's people 44; nicknames 48, 49; perspective, an evidence-based business model 17; response to situations 37
chemical engineering sector, case study Group's purpose 10
client installations: former regime's policy for responding to incidents 68; proactive and collaborative 68–69
client satisfaction: fundamental shift to excellent 70; from threatened litigation to 69–70
code of values 34; rationale in 35, **35–36**
codes of ethics 33
communication: radical staff engagement through face-to-face communication 46; staff engagement and 45–51, 47; two-way 19
Companies Act (2006), Section 172(1) of 92
company: core business process model 28; large-scale research of 15; leading and operating 24–25; nature of 2; non-believer 101; resolution for 100–102
company investment valuation 96–97
company purpose 2, 3, 6, 18; actualisation of 22; balance and integrate delivery of 86–88; defined as 56; middle management and company's people relationship 19; need to redefine 7–10; non-financial and financial metrics for assessing 101–102; root cause of 5, *95*, 95–97; *see also* purpose
company value investment 96
compliance: enabling subprocesses 33–36, **35–36**; proactive compliance decision 39; reactive compliance decision 38; subprocess 23–24
compliance-driven business 33
core business process model 15–16, 18, 22, 24, 28, 36, 56; of leading

and operating with heightened integrity 88
Corporation Purpose Ranking Index 94
Country Development Route Map 61
country offices: closure and redundancies 63; closure, South Africa 64; empowering, US 64–65; management and staff in 61; resulting specialisation of 62
customer and supplier relationships, complexity of 68
customer service 82

Dalio, Ray 1
decentralisation 81–82
delivery subprocesses 18–20; leadership 36–45
Deloitte 94
'Development Check' 52
Drucker, Peter 15

Edmans, A. 7, 18, 94; capitalism 12; defines company purpose 9; financial performance by 19
empowering country offices 64–65
enabling subprocesses: integrity/compliance 33–36, **35–36**; purpose statement 28–31; stakeholders 31–33, **32**
equity ownership 13
ethics 33, 34
evidence-based business model 2, 17

face-to-face communication, radical staff engagement through 46
feedback loop: challenging questions to CEO in open Q&A forum 54; between leaders and company's people 51–55, **53**; positive 52; rating of processes for closing 52, 53; subprocess 24
financial capital 4, 13, 86, 88
financial performance 1, 19, 93, 97
Financial Reporting Council (FRC) 92, 93
Fink, Larry 91
five behavioural principles 4, 14, 56, 82, 101
free market capitalism 1, 95
Friedman, Milton 1
FTSE corporations 93

Gallup 94
Generation Z 94
'golden nuggets' 47, 48
Good Business Charter 91
Google 97
governance 13, 18–20
Great Place to Work Institute's work
    20; individual company level for
    purpose-driven 15; survey 19–20,
    78–80, 83
GSK 8, 90; purpose statements 9–10
Guiso, L. 20
Gulf of Mexico Deepwater Horizon
    oil spill 83

Hamworthy Combustion Group 3–4,
    26–27; annual communications
    programme 45, 47; challenging and
    ambitious purpose 86; complex
    circumstances and environment
    104–106; Country Development
    Route Map 61; decisions and
    actions having adverse impact
    on people 63; delivery of 88–89;
    delivery subprocesses 36–55;
    enabling subprocesses 28–36;
    former management's regime 34;
    individuals facing exceptional
    personal problems 75–76; market
    sectors and growth drivers 103,
    104, 104; portfolio business
    model 107–110, 109, 110; prior
    people culture 57, 58; proactive
    and relentless commitment 89;
    purpose and profitability trade-off
    30; purpose and vision, business
    fundamentals for positioning
    delivery 106, 107; purpose of 29,
    103; sea change in people, 90th
    anniversary book 75
hard assets 96
heightened integrity 20–22, 24; case
    study corporation with 26; core
    business process model of leading
    and operating with 88; culture of
    89, 97; embedded culture of 79
Heightened Integrity Model 3–5,
    22–25, 23, 28, 51, 62, 66, 78, 83,
    84, 103, 106; demonstration and
    verification of 100–101; for leading
    and operating purpose-defined
    company 56

higher-profitability budget 30–31
human capital 4, 87
human resource (HR) services 31

informed feedback 24, 51
innovation 81
in-principle application 4
intangible asset 80, 81, 84, 97
integrity: definition of 21; enabling
    subprocesses 33–36, 35–36;
    subprocess 23–24
'Integrity Action' 52, 55n1
integrity-building approach: proactive
    compliance decision 39; proactive
    integrity decision 41–42; reactive
    compliance decision 38; reactive
    integrity decision 40
integrity-driven regime 33
intellectual capital 4, 87
internet-based virtual private network
    57, 58

Knowledge Bank 57, 59, 81; employee
    empowerment via 57, 59–60;
    empowering individual employees
    by 57–59
Kohneman, Daniel 53

leadership subprocess 24
leadership team: and pilot airing 35;
    set of values 34–35
leaders/leadership: CEOs, formal
    interaction across Group 42, 43;
    chairman's and vice chairman's,
    informal interaction across Group
    43; communicating processes
    between people and 24; and
    company's people interaction
    19; to create culture 21; delivery
    subprocesses 36–45; feedback
    loop between company's people
    and 51–55, 53; and personal
    accountability 57; proactive
    compliance decision 39; proactive
    integrity decision 41–42; proactive
    interaction of 55; reactive
    compliance decision 38; reactive
    integrity decision 40; two-way
    interaction between employees and
    45
legislation 13, 17, 76, 77, 90–91;
    purpose-based 92–93

Lewis, M. 53
long-term sustainable performance
  86, 88

management: in country offices 61
management control processes 47, 48
market leadership 73
Mayer, C. 7, 102n1; capitalism 12;
  defines company purpose 9; under-
  performance of UK economy 13;
  'Why' and 'What' of purpose 17
measurable business payoffs 4, 13,
  80–82, 101–102
middle management 19, 45;
  interaction between Group's people
  and 44
Millennials 1, 5, 93, 96, 97
moral leadership framework 18

natural capital 4, 86–87
nature: of CEOs 99; of company 1, 2,
  7–10; of interaction 44
nicknames 48, 49
non-believer companies 101
not-for-profit organisation 91
'Nudge Unit' 99

off-balance sheet assets 96
open consumer feedback process 51,
  52
operational performance 25, 69, 71,
  80
overall workplace quality 19, 20

performance 13, 18–20
personal accountability 14, 57
portfolio business model 107–110,
  109, 110
positive feedback loops 52
private equity owners 30
private investors 1, 91
proactive compliance decision 37, 39
proactive integrity-based feedback
  loop 53
proactive integrity decision 37, 41–42
pro-integrity business model 52
Project Dragonfly 97
purpose: behavioural principles
  56–78; of case study corporation
  10; of company 2, 3, 5, 7–10;
  definition for 7; Great Place
  to Work for Institute 78–80;
  Hamworthy Combustion Group 29;

measurable business payoffs 80–82;
  'Why' and the 'What' of 17; wider
  applicability of the model 82–84;
  see also company purpose
purpose-based legislation 92–93
purpose-defined agenda 7, 100
purpose-defined company 2–5, 31,
  100; characteristics 20; excellent
  customer service 82; with
  heightened integrity 21; Heightened
  Integrity Model for 56
purpose-driven business, five
  principles of 101
purpose-driven company 8, 17, 90,
  93; behavioural engagement and
  operational aspects of 31; modus
  operandi of 21; principles of 12
purpose-driven corporate agenda 5
purpose-driven portfolio business
  model 109–110
purpose statement: enabling
  subprocesses 28–31; subprocess
  22–23; Unilever and GSK 9–10
PwC/AIESEC study 94

ranking 93–94
R&D activities 29, 71
R&D facilities: strategy of investment
  in 71, 72; substantial investment in
  71, 73
R&D investment, substantial financial
  returns from 74
reactive compliance decision 37, 38
reactive integrity decision 37, 40
regulatory fines 13, 80, 82
resilience 13, 80, 82
resolution: for company 100–102; for
  society 99–100
responsible and responsive employer
  56, 57, 66, 82–83
right of reply 24, 52
RSB banking group 90
Rubik's cube 108, 110n1

Sapienza, P. 20
sense of shared responsibility 70, 77
shareholders 88, 90, 91, 93
shareholder value 1, 2, 91, 95, 96;
  primacy of 1, 90, 97, 99
social capital 4, 87–88
society: benefits for 86–89; business
  reconnecting with 99; resolution for
  99–100

South Africa, country offices closure 64
staff: in country offices 61;
    delivery subprocesses 45–51, 47;
    empowered to make decisions 34;
    proactive integrity-based feedback
    loop between management and
    53; productivity 80; recruitment,
    retention and motivation of
    81; subprocess 24; terms and
    conditions, transformation of
    31, **32**; turnover reductions and
    financial returns increases 48, 50
staff engagement, and communication
    45–51, 47
stakeholders 1, 5, 84, 88, 92;
    enabling subprocesses 31–33, **32**;
    subprocess 23
superior share price performance 13, 80

tangible asset 80; value of 96
taxation 96
Tech titans 84
third-party assessment 93–94
third-party best practice 4, 56, 83,
    84, 100
trade-off 31; purpose and
    profitability 30
transfer pricing policy 76–77

transparency 51, 53
Transparency International 93
transparent feedback 51
Tversby, Amos 53
two-game strategy 108–109, *110*
two-way communication 19

UK: believer companies 90; economy
    12–13, 102n1; Good Business
    Charter 91; legislative changes to
    corporate reporting requirements 92
Unilever 8, 90; purpose statements
    9–10
US: Benefit Corporations 90–91
user loyalty, generate 51–52
utilitarianism 7

values 15, 34; and beliefs 93;
    intergenerational shift in 5, 95; of
    tangible assets 96
values-based approach 45

workplace quality 19, 20, 79
'workplace quality score' 19–20
wrap-around value-added services
    108–109

Zingales, L. 20

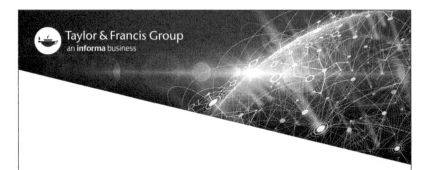

Taylor & Francis Group
an **informa** business

Taylor & Francis eBooks

www.taylorfrancis.com

A single destination for eBooks from Taylor & Francis
with increased functionality and an improved user
experience to meet the needs of our customers.

90,000+ eBooks of award-winning academic content in
Humanities, Social Science, Science, Technology, Engineering,
and Medical written by a global network of editors and authors.

TAYLOR & FRANCIS EBOOKS OFFERS:

A streamlined
experience for
our library
customers

A single point
of discovery
for all of our
eBook content

Improved
search and
discovery of
content at both
book and
chapter level

REQUEST A FREE TRIAL
support@taylorfrancis.com

 Routledge
Taylor & Francis Group

 CRC Press
Taylor & Francis Group

Printed in the United States
by Baker & Taylor Publisher Services